Poem-Making

Ways to Begin
Writing Poetry

POEM-MAKING

Ways to Begin Writing Poetry

Myra Cohn Livingston

A Charlotte Zolotow Book

An Imprint of HarperCollins*Publishers*

Poem-Making: Ways to Begin Writing Poetry
Copyright © 1991 by Myra Cohn Livingston
All rights reserved. No part of this book may be used or reproduced
in any manner whatsoever without written permission except in the
case of brief quotations embodied in critical articles and reviews.
Printed in the United States of America. For information address
HarperCollins Children's Books, a division of HarperCollins Publishers,
10 East 53rd Street, New York, NY 10022.
Typography by Al Cetta
3   4   5   6   7   8   9   10

Library of Congress Cataloging-in-Publication Data
Livingston, Myra Cohn.
    Poem-making : ways to begin writing poetry/Myra Cohn Livingston.
        p.   cm.
    "A Charlotte Zolotow book."
    Includes bibliographical references and index.
    Summary: Introduces the different kinds of poetry and the
mechanics of writing poetry, providing an opportunity for the reader
to experience the joy of making a poem.
    ISBN 0-06-024019-9. — ISBN 0-06-024020-2 (lib. bdg.)
    1. Poetry—Authorship—Study and teaching (Elementary)—Juvenile
literature.   2. Creative writing—Study and teaching (Elementary)—
Juvenile literature.   [1. Poetry—Authorship.   2. Creative
writing.]   I. Title.
LB1576.L578   1991   90-5012
372.6' 23—dc20   CIP
                                                          AC

To Jennifer Lee Factor because . . .

and with thanks to Bob Hendershot of Wyoming, Michigan,
who suggested the title

Contents

Contents

Introduction

IMAGINE that you've been spending the last few minutes watching a blue jay hide a cache of seeds in a tile roof. Or imagine that yesterday, out on a walk, you passed a dog barking angrily at you. Or think about a special time when you learned to roller-skate, the first time you went to the circus, or a day when a friend moved away.

All of these events are part of life—yours and mine—and when they happen there is always something inside of me that wants to turn what I see or hear or feel into a poem. The picture stays in my mind long after the blue jay has flown away or the dog stops barking. I begin to search for the words that will form themselves to make a picture I can share with others, the words that will re-create the experience for someone else.

This book is about poem-making, how to begin to understand what goes into a poem. We don't

ask the question *What* does a poem mean? for if
the poet has written well, we seem to know inside
of ourselves what it means to us. It is better to ask,
as John Ciardi has said, *How* does a poem mean?
And the *how* means writing the feeling in such a
special way that our listeners and readers can sense
something of what we have encountered, see something they might never have noticed before, or look
at something in a fresh way—the way the poet has
offered.

What we hope to do is to make the image, the
thought, even the sound come alive again. By arranging words, making a sort of music with these words,
we create something fascinating and new.

Poem-Making is an invitation for you to experience the joy of making a poem. It can be one of
the most exciting things you will ever learn to do!

—MCL
1991

Poem-Making
Ways to Begin
Writing Poetry

The Voices of Poetry

ONE DAY in a fifth-grade classroom I read to my students some poems about trees by James Reeves, Louis Simpson, Robert Frost, and Elizabeth Madox Roberts. Then we went outside to look at different trees and make notes.

When we returned, I suggested that we write poems about trees, those we had just seen or trees the students might know of at home or at camp, in Yosemite or Redwood National parks, or about a tree growing just outside the classroom window. It was my first day with this class, and I was pleased to see that they all began to write.

I have a habit of answering questions when I am teaching, walking around the classroom to see if anyone needs help. This day I noticed that many students were beginning their poems with "Some trees are tall, some trees are short" or "Trees are beautiful" or "I like trees." None of these beginnings,

3

understandably, seemed to inspire anyone to go further than one or two lines.

I remember this day particularly because it was the first time I had really thought about the *voices* of poetry and how, if used well, they could make all the difference in writing. I had been writing my own poetry, of course, never thinking about the voice I was using. But looking at these dull statements about trees and thinking about the poetry I had just read, I decided to try something new.

I asked one girl if she could tell me about a special tree she knew, just as Elizabeth Madox Roberts does in "Strange Tree."

> Away beyond the Jarboe house
> I saw a different kind of tree.
> Its trunk was old and large and bent
> And I could feel it look at me.

And the girl began "Over the fence I saw a tree," a poem that uses a *lyrical* voice, her own voice, telling something of her feelings about the tree.

I suggested to another girl that she walk to the window and look more carefully at the tree growing outside, its branches almost touching the building, and speak to it just as Robert Frost did when he wrote

Tree at my window, window tree,
My sash is lowered when night comes on;
But let there never be curtain drawn
Between you and me.

When this girl began to write "Come into the room, tree," she was using the dramatic voice of *apostrophe*. Other students in the class tried this voice, some asking their trees questions.

Five or six students wanted to try another dramatic voice, the *mask*, used by Louis Simpson in his poem "The Redwoods." It is a voice in which they pretend they are trees themselves speaking.

Mountains are moving, rivers
are hurrying. But we
are still.

We have the thoughts of giants—
clouds, and at night the stars . . .

Still others preferred to stay with the *narrative* voice, to simply tell about the trees without reference to themselves, as James Reeves does in "Tree Gowns."

In the morning her dress is of palest green,
And in dark green in the heat of noon is she seen . . .

No one used the dramatic voice of *conversation* that day. But it was an important day, because it taught me how to help students change dull, trite statements into far more interesting work. And the students taught me that they did not have to be in high school or college to understand the possibilities for expanding their writing, for entering into the magic of these five voices.

THE LYRICAL VOICE

A lyric poem is one that expresses the feelings and emotions of the poet. Originally such a poem was written to be sung to the music of a lyre. We carry over this idea by calling the words to our songs "lyrics."

The *lyrical* voice can be identified most often by the use of the personal pronouns *I*, *me*, *my*, *we*, *our*, and *us* or any related words—*mine*, *ours*. It is used to speak of personal experience, to comment on how the poet looks at the world. Emily Dickinson uses a lyrical voice in her poem:

> I never saw a moor,
> I never saw the sea;
> Yet know I how the heather looks,
> And what a wave must be.
>
> I never spoke with God,
> Nor visited in heaven;
> Yet certain am I of the spot
> As if the chart were given.

We cannot mistake this voice, for Emily Dickinson begins with the word "I."

Sometimes we must read further before we know who is speaking. Eloise Greenfield writes in "Aunt Roberta"

> What do people think about
> When they sit and dream
> All wrapped up in quiet
>   and old sweaters
> And don't even hear me 'til I
> Slam the door?

The pronouns "me" and "I" establish that this is indeed a lyric poem. Other poems of Eloise Greenfield begin "I get way down in the music" or "When my friend Lessie runs she runs so fast" or

> Went to the corner
> Walked in the store
> Bought me some candy

Christina Rossetti writes in this same voice when she asks

> Who has seen the wind?
>   Neither I nor you:
> But when the leaves hang trembling
>   The wind is passing thro'.

Who has seen the wind?
  Neither you nor I;
But when the trees bow down their heads
  The wind is passing by.

There are times however when the poet's voice
seems hidden, when we cannot find any personal
pronouns and yet we know by what is said that
the ideas in the poem are original with the writer.
Some personal observation is made that would not
be an ordinary way of seeing or hearing or thinking.

In her poem "Metaphor" Eve Merriam's particular
way of comparing morning to a new sheet of paper
tells us that this is her idea.

Morning is
a new sheet of paper
for you to write on.

Whatever you want to say,
all day,
until night
folds it up
and files it away.

The bright words and the dark words
are gone
until dawn
and a new day
to write on.

Although she never uses a personal pronoun, we know it is the poet who has made this metaphor.

Similarly, "Rain into River" tells us how X. J. Kennedy hears the rain, and how he observes it.

> Rain into river
> falling
>
> tingles
>
> one
> at
> a
> time
>
> the trout's
> tin shingles.

It should not be difficult to learn to recognize a lyric poem. Nor should it be difficult for you to use the lyrical voice. Each time you tell about yourself and your experiences, about your own observations and events of which you are a part, you will be writing a lyric poem.

This is the voice that most people use.

THE NARRATIVE VOICE

The *narrative* voice tells a story. It may be a story as simple as a nursery rhyme.

> Hey diddle diddle,
> The cat and the fiddle,
> The cow jumped over the moon;
> The little dog laughed
> To see such sport,
> And the dish ran away with the spoon.

It may be a humorous story such as Ogden Nash's "The Adventures of Isabel."

> Isabel met an enormous bear,
> Isabel, Isabel, didn't care;
> The bear was hungry, the bear was ravenous,
> The bear's big mouth was cruel and cavernous.
> The bear said, Isabel, glad to meet you,
> How do, Isabel, now I'll eat you!
> Isabel, Isabel, didn't worry,
> Isabel didn't scream or scurry,
> She washed her hands and she straightened her
> hair up,
> Then Isabel quietly ate the bear up.

11

A narrative poem may also be a long epic such as *The Odyssey* written by Homer, a Greek who lived sometime between 1200 and 850 B.C. Translated into English by Robert Fitzgerald, these lines describe the beginning of a boar hunt.

> When the young Dawn spread in the eastern sky
> her finger-tips of rose, the men and dogs
> went hunting, taking Odysseus. They climbed
> Parnassos' rugged flank mantled in forest,
> entering amid high windy folds at noon
> when Hêlios beat upon the valley floor
> and on the winding Ocean whence he came.
> With hounds questing ahead, in open order,
> the sons of Autólykos went down a glen,
> Odysseus in the lead, behind the dogs,
> pointing his long-shadowing spear.

Lewis Carroll begins his famous nonsense narrative "Jabberwocky" with these stanzas:

> 'Twas brillig, and the slithy toves
>   Did gyre and gimble in the wabe:
> All mimsy were the borogoves,
>   And the mome raths outgrabe.
>
> "Beware the Jabberwock, my son!
>   The jaws that bite, the claws that catch!
> Beware the Jubjub bird, and shun
>   The frumious Bandersnatch!"

He took his vorpal sword in hand:
  Long time the manxome foe he sought—
So rested he by the Tumtum tree,
  And stood awhile in thought. . . .

Whether you prefer a short nursery verse like "Hey Diddle Diddle"; a funny verse, "The Adventures of Isabel"; an epic, *The Odyssey*; or nonsense like "Jabberwocky," it's important to know that all of these are written in a narrative voice.

You probably know many narrative poems already. "Casey at the Bat" by Ernest Lawrence Thayer is one that tells about a disastrous ball game. Edward Lear has written in "The Owl and the Pussy Cat" about an owl and a cat who sail away to get married. Robert Browning told of a man who rid a town of rats and punished its greedy citizens in "The Pied Piper of Hamelin." The first story poems you may have heard were in *Mother Goose*. As you grow older, you will probably read stories told in poetry, such as Alfred, Lord Tennyson's *Idylls of the King* or "The Highwayman" by Alfred Noyes.

In all of these examples the poet-narrator recounts something that has happened. It is like a storyteller spinning a story. Whether the story comes out of the poet's imagination or, like a ballad (see the chapter on ballads), tells of an event that actually took place, poets are not a part of the story. They do not comment on it. They do not put themselves into the story as they would in a lyrical poem. They are somewhat like newscasters on television or radio announcers who merely tell you the facts or give you information.

Notice the first lines of these narrative poems:

Hey diddle diddle,
Isabel met an enormous bear,
When the young Dawn spread in the eastern sky
'Twas brillig, and the slithy toves

Poets seem to plunge right into their narratives, enabling both the words and the rhythms to indicate what kind of story it will be. Three of these examples immediately clue us in to the notion that they are either funny or nonsense. One is more serious. The poet sets a mood that pulls the reader into the story.

First you will need to decide what sort of narrative you wish to write. You may begin with something as nonsensical as "Hey diddle diddle," and yet your choice may surprise you. "Hey diddle diddle" is only one stanza, but a narrative like "Old Mother Hubbard" goes on for many, many stanzas.

You may use *couplets* as Ogden Nash does, or *quatrains* like Lewis Carroll. I doubt that you would want to attempt the complicated metrical patterns used by the Greeks, but you will certainly wish to create a rhythm and rhyme scheme that will help your narrative carry its idea across—a lighthearted meter if your verse is funny and another kind of metrical pattern for a serious poem. All of these forms and meters are discussed in later chapters.

It might help to spend some time reading other narrative poems. Lewis Carroll's "The Walrus and the Carpenter" is a good example of a long story poem. It includes the famous lines

> "The time has come," the Walrus said,
>   "To talk of many things;
> Of shoes—and ships—and sealing wax—
>   Of cabbages—and kings—
> And why the sea is boiling hot—
>   And whether pigs have wings."

Shel Silverstein's "Sarah Cynthia Sylvia Stout Would Not Take the Garbage Out" and "Jimmy Jet and His TV Set" are other examples of good narrative verse you may already know. If you don't know a story poem—a narrative poem or verse—that is meaningful to you, you can find many in poetry anthologies and begin to write one of your own.

THE DRAMATIC VOICE

Apostrophe

Do you ever talk to things that cannot answer? One day out in my garden I bent over to smell a rose when a bee zoomed down, almost daring me to go near the flower. It made me think

> Who has the better
> right to smell the first summer
> rose, bee—you or I?

I have talked not only to bees but to telephone lines, to a lemon tree, to winter, to spices, to mockingbirds, to the sky and sun and stars. A great deal of my poetry is written in the voice of *apostrophe*—a voice that addresses something that cannot answer.

You may remember, when you were very young, talking to the milk when it spilled, blaming it instead of yourself, or to your bicycle, or to something else that had no life of its own. Through the voice of apostrophe you spoke to it as though it were alive.

Poets know how powerful this voice can be and

use it in many ways. In her poem "Moon" Karla
Kuskin asks

> Moon
> Have you met my mother?
> Asleep in a chair there
> Falling down hair.
>
> Moon in the sky
> Moon in the water
> Have you met one another?
> Moon face to moon face
> Deep in that dark place
> Suddenly bright.
>
> Moon
> Have you met my friend the night?

Some of my favorite poems are written in the
voice of apostrophe. Robert Frost speaks to a tree
in a poem called "Tree at My Window." Carl Sandburg, in a poem to a bluebird, asks the bluebird
what it feeds on. Hilda Conkling speaks to a "Mouse."

> Little mouse in gray velvet,
> Have you had a cheese-breakfast?
> There are no crumbs on your coat,
> Did you use a napkin?
> I wonder what you had to eat,
> And who dresses you in gray velvet?

And in "Go Wind" Lilian Moore tells the wind what
to do.

> Go wind, blow
> Push wind, swoosh.
> > Shake things
> > take things
> > make things
> > > fly.
>
> > Ring things
> > swing things
> > fling things
> > > high.
>
> Go wind, blow
> Push things——wheee.
> > No, wind, no.
> > Not me—
> > not *me*.

Christina Rossetti addresses a caterpillar.

> Brown and furry
> Caterpillar in a hurry
> Take your walk
> To the shady leaf, or stalk,
> Or what not,
> Which may be the chosen spot.
> No toad spy you,

Hovering bird of prey pass by you;
Spin and die,
To live again a butterfly.

These poems are written in many different forms. One is written in free verse. One is written in quatrains. Two are written in couplets. Later I'll discuss these forms, but now look on page 114 and find a cinquain I wrote to a T-shirt.

Try looking around you at this moment. Choose something of which you might ask a question or to which you might tell something. Use whatever form seems best to you. And remember when you want to write a poem, the voice of apostrophe is often the very best voice for wondering, asking questions, or giving a bit of advice!

The Mask

When my daughter was very young, we had to call her Sailor Nine. Her real name is Jennie, but she wouldn't answer unless we addressed her as Sailor Nine. Perhaps you pretended you were a ballerina or an astronaut or someone other than yourself. Poets *never* stop imagining what it might be like to be not only another person, but even something that cannot, in reality, think or speak.

This aspect of the dramatic voice is what I think of as a *mask* or *persona*. It is as though we put on the face or the body of someone or something else and tell about ourselves through our words. Lilian Moore puts on a mask—or persona—to write "Message from a Caterpillar."

> Don't shake this
> bough.
> Don't try
> to wake me
> now.

In this cocoon
I've work to
do.
Inside this silk
I'm changing
things.

I'm worm-like now
but in this
dark
I'm growing
wings.

A Papago Indian poem uses an animal mask in "Song of the Deer."

Here I come forth.
On the earth I fell over:
The snapping bow made me dizzy.

Here I come forth.
On the mountain I slipped:
The humming arrow made me dizzy.

Perhaps you imagine, as I do, that almost anything can have a life of its own. When I visit Monterey, California, I see a gnarled, windswept tree known as the Monterey cypress. Once, looking at its strange, tortured shape, I turned myself into the tree and wrote

                  at whim of winds
                          my limbs are bent
                  to grotesque shape
                      by element
                          of ocean spray
                              and salty wind
                      and who may see
                              my bleached bole pinned
                                  into the sand
                                  shall
                                  wonder
                                  why
                                  I
                                      twist
                                      alive
                                      while
                                      others
                                          die

In this poem, called "Monterey Cypress: Pt. Lobos,"
I not only used a mask but tried to indicate the
shape of the cypress by the way the lines are placed.

   "The Snowflake" by Walter de la Mare is one of
my favorite poems.

            Before I melt,
            Come, look at me!
            This lovely icy filigree!
            Of a great forest

In one night
I make a wilderness
Of white:
By skyey cold
Of crystals made,
All softly, on
Your finger laid,
I pause, that you
My beauty see:
Breathe, and I vanish
Instantly.

When I teach classes, I ask students to use the mask, to pretend to be something else. Some like to think of themselves as whirlwinds, tornadoes, or strong mountains. Others choose to pretend they are beautiful flowers. I will never forget one fifth-grade boy who wrote of himself as a lonely root. It was a very good poem, because he was indeed a lonely person who chose the right inanimate object to tell something about the way he felt.

The use of the mask can turn an ordinary sort of statement into a wonderful poem. Imagine that someone has decided to tell about a seashell and writes

A sea-shell is washed up by the ocean.
No one picks it up, or listens to it.
No one hears its song.

How much more fascinating this is when Geoffrey
Scott in his poem "Frutta di Mare (Fruits of the
Sea)" pretends he is a shell.

> I am a sea-shell flung
> Up from the ancient sea;
> Now I lie here, among
> Roots of a tamarisk tree;
> No one listens to me.
>
> I sing to myself all day
> In a husky voice, quite low,
> Things the great fishes say
> And you most need to know;
> All night I sing just so.
>
> But lift me from the ground,
> And hearken at my rim,
> Only your sorrow's sound,
> Amazed, perplexed and dim,
> Comes coiling to the brim,
>
> For what the wise whales ponder
> Awaking from sleep,
> The key to all your wonder,
> The answers to the deep,
> These to myself I keep.

Norma Farber has written poems in which she
pretends to be a turtle or a caterpillar. Harry Behn
imagines himself as a river and Carl Sandburg be-

comes a pumpkin. You will find many poems that use this voice in anthologies, for poets never feel too old to pretend.

Look around you and find something inanimate: a chair, a table, perhaps a piece of fruit or some food. You might want to be a baseball, a skateboard, or a yo-yo. Think of what you might say if you could talk, a question you might ask, or a secret you have never told anyone before now. Like Lilian Moore's caterpillar you may want to begin with a warning. Or you might ask your reader to look at you before you vanish like Walter de la Mare's snowflake. You will find something in your own experience that may suddenly ask you to give it life and a voice. And of course you will!

Conversation

In addition to apostrophe and mask, the dramatic voice often uses *conversation*. Heard as a dialogue between two voices, it may remind us of listening to a radio, attending the theater, or watching and hearing several people speak on television. In this old nursery rhyme

> What's the news of the day,
> Good neighbor, I pray?
> They say the balloon
> Is gone up to the moon.

there are two voices. The first clue is the use of "good neighbor" in the second line, so we know someone is speaking to a neighbor. The third and fourth lines are the answer, which we also assume to be that of the speaker's neighbor.

In "Vermont Conversation" Patricia Hubbell writes

> "Good weather for hay."
>   "Yes, 'tis."
> "Mighty bright day."
>   "That's true."
> "Crops comin' on?"
>   "Yep. You?"

"Tol'rable; beans got the blight."
    "Way o' the Lord."
"That's right."

Here are two voices, taking alternating lines. Patricia Hubbell tells us in the title that this is taking place in Vermont. A clue about the speakers occurs in lines 5 and 7, when we learn that "crops" and "beans" must identify them as farmers. In addition, the terseness and spareness of the sentences remind us that people in Vermont do not usually waste words.

    Poets often clue us in. Here is John Drinkwater's "Snail."

> Snail upon the wall,
> Have you got at all
> Anything to tell
> About your shell?
>
> Only this, my child—
> When the wind is wild,
> Or when the sun is hot,
> It's all I've got.

Not only the title but the first word in the poem identifies that someone is speaking to a snail. In the fourth line, when the snail answers, we learn that the speaker is a "child."

    One of my favorite conversation poems is "Old Man Ocean" by Russell Hoban.

Old Man Ocean, how do you pound
Smooth glass rough, rough stones round?
Time and the tide and the wild waves rolling,
Night and the wind and the long gray dawn.

Old Man Ocean, what do you tell,
What do you sing in the empty shell?
Fog and the storm and the long bell tolling,
Bones in the deep and the brave men gone.

Here the ocean's reply is identified by the use of italics and indentation, a technique that helps us to read the poem easily.

One conversation poem I have written happened because I remembered, from my junior high school days when I studied journalism, the five rules of a news story. One must always ask who, what, where, when, and why. In the 1970's the government decided to celebrate George Washington's birthday on a day other than February 22, which bothered me because I always think birthdays should be celebrated on the right day. So I imagined a conversation with the "Father of Our Country" and called the poem "Conversation with Washington."

They did it, George. They did it.
What?
They changed your birthday quite a lot.
How?

They moved it to another day.
>   *Why?*

So they could have more time to play.
>   *Where?*

At lakes or mountains, or just rest—
>   *When?*

Some time ago. They thought it best.
>   *Who?*

Your children, George. They thought that you
Would understand. (Most fathers do—)

Not all poems that use conversation are written
in the dramatic voice. Ralph Waldo Emerson begins
"Fable" with

> The mountain and the squirrel
> Had a quarrel,
> And the former called the latter, "Little Prig;"
> Bun replied,
> "You are doubtless big . . ."

George MacDonald's poem "The Wind and the
Moon" is another example of a poem using conversation.

> Said the Wind to the Moon, "I will blow you out;
> You stare
> In the air
> Like a ghost in a chair,

Always looking what I am about—
I hate to be watched; I'll blow you out."

Yet both of these poems are narrative poems, introduced by phrases that tell readers who or what is
speaking.

Dramatic conversational poems often allow us to
guess, almost as if we are reading a riddle, who
the speakers may be. This kind of conversational
poem may be a natural outgrowth of the use of
apostrophe, as if the poet is speaking to something
and then realizing that an answer is required. The
poem you choose to write might stop with the com-
ments or questions you have—or it might go on
to take the form of conversation. It is up to you to
decide which is the best!

Sound and Rhyme

To MANY people *rhyme* is a necessary part of poetry. To others it is an artificial way of writing. Attitudes toward rhyme depend on how one thinks about poetry, whether or not the music it creates is pleasant or forced. A good rhyme, a repetition of sounds, pleases us. It gives a certain order to our thoughts and settles in the ears pleasantly. If you believe, as I do, that music is an important part of poetry, rhyme can be a wonderful tool. But used poorly, rhyme is not only ridiculous but sometimes keeps us from saying what we wish to say.

Once during a writing workshop I asked my students to observe a tall black lamp in a garden and write about it. One girl said this:

> Lamps are on
> Some stay on all night
> for people to see
> because they give off light

> When you are alone
> it keeps you capone

This use of rhyme is an example of how the reader is cut off from knowing what the poet wants to say—in this case, how the girl felt about being alone in the dark. What she might have written is how she felt when she was alone. Instead she made up a word just for the sake of rhyme. This is a poor use of rhyme.

Sometimes beginning writers use rhyme so often that it ceases to be meaningful and just becomes boring.

> Love is nice
> and so are mice
> I like rice
> and I like spice
> I like ice
> and I like dice . . .

Long ago I wrote a poem about roller-skating. Thinking of how smoothly I skated down a hilly street when I was ten years old, I tried to catch the rhythm and the constant downward motion by using a falling rhythm and rhyme in "Skating Song."

Never stopping
Once you've gone,
Never looking
At the lawn,
Whizzing down
From crack to crack,
April whistling
At your back.
Spinning wheels
On bumpy ground,
Sidewalks sing
A hollow sound.
Over stones and twigs and holes,
Over mud and sticks and poles,
Past the houses,
Past the trees,
Swinging arms and bending knees,
Past the fence posts,
Past the gates,
Here we come
On roller skates.

One day, however, when I watched my young
daughter trying to learn how to roller-skate, I wrote
"74th Street":

Hey, this little kid gets roller skates.
She puts them on.
She stands up and almost

flops over backwards.
She sticks out a foot like
she's going somewhere and
falls down and
smacks her hand. She
grabs hold of a step to get up and
sticks out the other foot and
slides about six inches and
falls and
skins her knee.

                    And then, you know what?

She brushes off the dirt and the
blood and puts some
spit on it and then
sticks out the other foot

              again.

My daughter starting, then falling, then starting again
with many kinds of movements inspired a different
sort of poem. I tried to catch her irregular movements
in the irregular sounds and meter of the poem. The
words, the sound of them, needed to fit the content
of what they said.

Some writers use rhyme more easily than others;
their patterns flow naturally into its use. Others find
it difficult. But a well-done rhyme adds a musical

appeal to a poem. Rhyme also helps us remember
a poem more easily.

Rhyming patterns in poetry form into groups that
we call *stanzas*. Sometimes one stanza can be an
entire poem, as in "Discovery."

> Round and round and round I spin,
> Making a circle so I can fall in.

A stanza may have two, three, four, five, six, seven,
eight, or nine lines or even more. There are two
stanzas in Christina Rossetti's poem

> The horses of the sea
>   Rear a foaming crest,
> But the horses of the land
>   Serve us the best.
>
> The horses of the land
>   Munch corn and clover,
> While the foaming sea-horses
>   Toss and turn over.

Some poets always write in stanzas. Others put
their stanzas together. How this is decided depends
on the sense of the poem and what is being said.
In "Skating Song" all the stanzas are together because

when people are skating, they are not likely to stop once they have built up the momentum of going down a hill.

Stanzas have special names, depending on the number of lines.

Two lines	Couplet
Three lines	Tercet
Four lines	Quatrain
Five lines	Quintet
Six lines	Sestet
Seven lines	Septet
Eight lines	Octave

A stanza of nine lines or more is known simply as a nine-line stanza, a ten-line stanza, and so on.

Longer stanzas, as you will learn, are made up of variations on couplets, tercets, and quatrains. These three are often called the "building blocks" of poetry, so it is important to understand how they work.

It would be a good idea to start with the couplet, then go on to the tercet and quatrain. In my classes we spend a week or two learning each stanza form before going on to the next. Writing poems in a form over and over helps students to learn that pattern so well that they never forget it.

You can set your own timetable, and when you're certain you know a pattern, begin a new one—all the way from two lines up to nine or ten or twelve or fourteen or even more!

COUPLETS, TERCETS, AND QUATRAINS

The *couplet* is not only one of the oldest rhyming forms but one that pleases the ear. We write a line "One, two" and immediately search for a rhythm and sound to balance our words. "Buckle my shoe." We say "Rain, rain, go away" and are satisfied when we complete both the image and the pattern with "Come again another day."

A couplet is two lines that rhyme, one after the other, usually equal in length. Sometimes a couplet can be a complete poem, as in William Jay Smith's "The Mirror."

> I look in the Mirror, and what do I see?
> A little of you, and a lot of me!

When one couplet makes a complete poem, it is called a *closed couplet*.

Often we find poems that use two couplets, one following the other. In his book *Opposites* Richard Wilbur writes

38

The opposite of *doughnut*? Wait
A minute while I meditate.

This isn't easy. Ah, I've found it!
A cookie with a hole around it.

John Ciardi in "It Makes No Difference to Me" uses three couplets.

I climbed a mountain three feet high
And banged my head against the sky.

"Watch out!" my sister's brother said.
"You climb that high, you'll lose your head!"

I didn't care. Mine is no use
To anyone. What's your excuse?

Just as couplets are groups of two lines that rhyme with each other, the *tercet* is a group of three lines that may be put together in varying patterns.

The first of these is a form that uses only one end sound, as Ogden Nash does in "The Eel."

I don't mind eels
Except as meals
And the way they feels.

Tercets that use only one end rhyme sound are called triplets.

In her poem "Firefly" Elizabeth Madox Roberts
writes

> A little light is going by,
> Is going up to see the sky,
> A little light with wings.
>
> I never could have thought of it,
> To have a little bug all lit
> And made to go on wings.

Here there are two rhyming patterns (by/sky and
it/lit) with the word "wings" repeated in both stanzas
to hold the tercet together. Another tercet pattern
is found in David McCord's "This Is My Rock."

> This is my rock,
> And here I run
> To steal the secret of the sun;
>
> This is my rock
> And here come I
> Before the night has swept the sky;
>
> This is my rock,
> This is the place
> I meet the evening face to face.

Here the second and third lines in each stanza rhyme.
Sometimes tercets are written so that the first and

third lines rhyme. David McCord begins his poem "Father and I in the Woods" with the stanza

> "Son,"
> My father used to say,
> "Don't run."

Of all the rhyming forms in poetry the *quatrain* is probably the most widely used. Quatrain takes its name from the French for "four," *quatre*. This stanza is made up of four lines and comes in many different patterns.

Most often a quatrain will rhyme the second line with the fourth, as in the old verse

> As I was standing in the street,
> As quiet as could be,
> A great big ugly man came up
> And tied his horse to me.

Another popular form is the use of two couplets, one after the other, as Lucille Clifton writes in "July."

> Everett Anderson thinks he'll make
> America a birthday cake
> Only the sugar's almost gone
> and payday's not till later on.

A more difficult but common form is one in which both the first and third lines and the second and fourth lines rhyme. This pattern is found in Lewis Carroll's "Father William," which begins

"You are old, Father William," the young man said,
   "And your hair has become very white;
And yet you incessantly stand on your head—
   Do you think, at your age, it is right?"

"In my youth," Father William replied to his son,
   "I feared it might injure the brain;
But now that I'm perfectly sure I have none,
   Why, I do it again and again."

Here the rhymes said/head, white/right, son/none, and brain/again add to the musical appeal of the verses.

Still another quatrain pattern can be found in Shel Silverstein's "The Flying Festoon."

Oh, I'm going to ride on the Flying Festoon—
I'll jump on his back and I'll whistle a tune,
And we'll fly to the outermost tip of the moon,
         The Flying Festoon and I.

I'm taking a sandwich, and ball and a prune,
And we're leaving this evening precisely at noon,
For I'm going to fly with The Flying Festoon . . .
         Just as soon as he learns how to fly.

Another pattern is found in this old nursery rhyme:

> Cock a doodle do!
> My dame has lost her shoe,
> My master's lost his fiddlestick
> And knows not what to do.

The only line that does not rhyme here is the third.
    Still another way to write a quatrain can be seen in Alfred, Lord Tennyson's "The Kraken."

> About his shadowy sides: above him swell
> Huge sponges of millennial growth and height;
> And far away into the sickly light
> From many a wondrous grot and secret cell.

Two rhyming lines surrounded by two other rhyming lines, as though they were enclosed, is called *envelope* verse.
    Couplets, tercets, and quatrains have many variations and may be used by themselves, or may be put together in other combinations to make longer poems. This variety of patterns allows poets to find the best way for them to express what they would like to say in their poems.

LONGER STANZAS

Once you've learned to write couplets, tercets, and quatrains, you may wish to try poems with longer stanzas of five, six, seven, eight, or even more lines. There are many of these patterns, and some with special names.

In the *quintet*, or five-line stanza, you might try starting with a couplet and then adding a tercet, just as David McCord does in his poem "Cocoon."

> The little caterpillar creeps
> Awhile before in silk it sleeps.
> It sleeps awhile before it flies,
> And flies awhile before it dies,
> And that's the end of three good tries.

Next you might try reversing the pattern, using the tercet first with the couplet following. Emily Dickinson wrote

> To make a prairie it takes a clover and one bee,
> One clover and one bee,
> And revery.
> The revery alone will do
> If bees are few.

44

Six-line stanzas, or *sestets*, can be made up of three couplets, a couplet and a quatrain, two tercets, or other patterns. You may wish to start with successive couplets, as in Theodore Roethke's "The Ceiling."

> Suppose the Ceiling went Outside
> And then caught Cold and Up and Died?
> The only Thing we'd have for Proof
> That he was Gone, would be the Roof;
> I think it would be most Revealing
> To find out how the Ceiling's Feeling.

Russell Hoban has two tercets in "The Crow."

> Flying loose and easy, where does he go
> Swaggering in the sky, what does he know,
> Why is he laughing, the carrion crow?
> Why is he shouting, why won't he sing,
> How did he steal them, whom will he bring
> Loaves of blue heaven under each wing?

You might also begin your sestet with a quatrain and end with a couplet, or try a form of envelope verse where the first and sixth lines rhyme, the second and fifth lines rhyme, and the third and fourth lines rhyme. Here is the beginning of "The Turtle":

We found him down at Turtle Creek,
Reached in the water and pulled him out,
His back all sticky with muck and slime.
We didn't take him home that time
But Saturday he was still about
So we brought him home. It's been a week. . . .

Seven-line stanzas, called *septets*, can be made up of quatrains and tercets, while eight-line stanzas, *octaves*, might be four couplets, or two tercets and a couplet, or two quatrains. You might also want to try using a couplet at the beginning and one at the end with a quatrain in the middle.

For longer stanzas you can follow any pattern you like. In his poem "Camel," William Jay Smith writes

The Camel is a long-legged humpbacked beast
With the crumpled-up look of an old worn shoe.
He walks with a creep and a slouch and a slump
As over the desert he carries his hump
Like a top-heavy ship, like a bumper bump-bump.
See him plodding in caravans out of the East,
Bringing silk for a party and dates for a feast.
Is he tired? Is he *thirsty*? No, not in the least.
Good morning, Sir Camel! Good morning to you!

The pattern of this poem, William Jay Smith explains, just happened because of the thoughts that went through his head. After writing the first two lines to explain how the camel looks, he began to describe its movements, and the idea of "hump" carried over to the movement "bump-bump." Then to explain further about the locale of the "East" and what he brought, he carried on the rhyme for another two lines, ending with not only the actual confrontation of meeting a camel but also what he might say to him. Listening to his poem, we hear that he could not leave the sound of the second line in the air, and so he rhymed *shoe* and *you*, which not only completes the sense but satisfies the ear.

This is another example of *how* a poem means, and what helps us, when we are writing poetry, to know what to do. We do not often say that we are setting about to write three tercets or two quatrains. The subject of the poem offers us new ways to write, and we experiment with the forms.

Remember that often the same end-rhyme sound can be used in every line, or each few lines may have a different end sound. You may want to try some of the patterns mentioned or make up your own patterns. Notice when you are reading poetry how poets put their stanzas together. Sometimes you may wish to imitate their patterns, for when we begin anything, we learn through imitation. Later on we feel confident enough to experiment.

Most important, you'll find that sometimes the idea, the thought you have, leads you into a pattern without your choosing it beforehand. This is part of the surprise and excitement of making a poem.

Sometimes when I get an idea, I quickly write down all my thoughts and even some lines or phrases. When I put these together, I recognize where my patterns or lines have gone off—why it doesn't look or sound right. If you've learned the basic patterns—the couplet, tercet, and quatrain—you will be able to do this too.

THE BALLAD

If you enjoy listening to rousing stories told in verse (and most people do), you'll want to know more about *ballads*. Folk ballads are the oldest type of poetry we know. Long before radio, television, or movies, in days when most people didn't know how to read, wandering storytellers would bring the news in rhyme and verse. Often ballads were set to music and sung.

Originally ballads were not written down, but passed from one person to another, one generation to the next, through oral tradition. Later they were collected and are still collected by scholars who write them down or record them.

Many versions are to be found of the same ballad. Each time a ballad was sung or recited, it changed according to what someone remembered of it. The first time I heard the ballad "John Henry," it began

John Henry was a little baby,
Sitting on his mama's knee,
Said, "The Big Bend Tunnel on the C. & O. Road
Is gonna be the death of me,
    Lawd, gonna be the death of me."

Later I heard this beginning:

> When John Henry was a little babe,
> A-holding to his daddy's hand,
> Says, "If I live till I'm twenty-one,
> I'm going to make a steel-driving man, yes sir,
> Going to make a steel-driving man."

Perhaps you know still another version, for all ballads are repeated in different ways. The oldest told tales of brave exploits, of love and death, of dark events, heroes and villains. Today many of our pop and country singers sing of current events, which they weave into stories.

Most ballads are anonymous: We do not know who wrote them. "The Fox" is such an American ballad.

> The fox went out on a chilly night,
> Prayed to the moon for to give him light,
> For he'd many a mile to go that night
>   Afore he reached the town-o.
>
> He ran till he came to a great big bin;
> The ducks and the geese were put therein.
> "A couple of you will grease my chin,
>   Afore I leave this town-o."

He grabbed the gray goose by the neck,
Throwed a duck across his back;
He didn't mind the "quack, quack, quack"
　　And the legs a-dangling down-o.

Then old mother Flipper-Flopper jumped out of bed,
Out of the window she stuck her head,
Crying "John! John! The gray goose is gone
　　And the fox is on the town-o!"

Then John, he went to the top of the hill,
Blowed his horn both loud and shrill;
The fox, he said, "I better flee with my kill
　　Or they'll soon be on my trail-o."

He ran till he came to his cozy den,
There were the little ones, eight, nine, ten.
They said, "Daddy, better go back again,
　　'Cause it must be a mighty fine town-o."

Then the fox and his wife without any strife,
Cut up the goose with a fork and a knife;
They never had such a supper in their life
　　And the little ones chewed on the bones-o.

A ballad has certain recognizable features. It describes some dramatic event, almost rushing through the story without attention to settings or detail. Action is important and is told in simple, direct, nonfigurative language. The true ballad stanza follows a simple quatrain pattern. Often there is a repetitive refrain.

In America, ballads have been composed about cowboys, railroad men, miners, sailors, war, disasters, and national and folk heroes. Most of us know ballads like "I Ride An Old Paint" or "Clementine" or "Yankee Doodle." Each of these ballads tells a specific story about some event or person.

You might wish to write a ballad telling about some occurrence in your own life or that of your family. If you sign it, however, you will be writing a literary ballad, which is often an imitation of the old anonymous form. John Keats did this when he wrote "La Belle Dame Sans Merci." Other sophisticated literary ballads have been written by Elizabeth Bishop in "The Ballad of the Burglar of Babylon" and Samuel Taylor Coleridge in "The Rime of the Ancient Mariner." There are many excellent anthologies with ballads you might enjoy reading.

It's a good idea to start with the quatrain stanza and then move on later to a more complicated form. You'll want to make sure that your ballad tells an exciting or interesting story. Perhaps there is some historical event in social studies that you could develop, such as the story of the Boston Tea Party, the voyages of Columbus, or a battle. You might also find a newspaper story that interests you. Once you obtain all the facts and write your ballad, you may wish to set it to music and perform it for your family and friends.

Other Elements of Sound

REPETITION

ANOTHER WAY in which sound works to hold a poem together is by the use of *repetition*. When rhyme or a strict metrical pattern is not used, a group of words may sound more like prose. Repetition—a word or phrase used several or even many times—helps to create a music. This does not mean that saying something over and over again will make a poem, but rather that a careful choice of words or phrases establishes a pattern that appeals to our ears.

In his "Poem" Langston Hughes writes

> I loved my friend.
> He went away from me.
> That's all there is to say.
> The poem ends
> Soft as it began.
> I loved my friend.

Here the first line "I loved my friend" repeated at the end not only ties the poem together but also emphasizes Hughes's love for his friend.

American Indian poetry uses a great deal of repetition. This Cherokee Indian poem, "Beware of Me!," relies on the use of repeated phrases for its rhythm, sense, and humor.

> i stand on the rock
> ho, bear!
> beware of me!
>
> i stand on the tree
> ho, eagle!
> beware of me!
>
> i stand on the mountain
> ho, enemy!
> beware of me!
>
> i stand in the camp
> ho, chiefs!
> beware of me!
>
> here comes a bee!
> i run and hide!
> he would sting me!

Phrases like "i stand on the" and "ho" both serve as pleasant repetitive and familiar patterns. The warning "beware of me!" repeated four times emphasizes the bravery that the speaker is supposedly feeling, shattered by the last stanza. Here repetition serves an important function by establishing the nature of the speaker's cowardly nature.

In her poem "The Song in My Head" Felice Holman writes

> The song in my head
> The song in my head
>   goes over
>   goes over
>   and over
> Sing me another
> Sing me another
> Sing me a song that will drive this one out
>   drive this one out
>   drive this one out. . . .

It is obvious here that repetition emphasizes what happens when we cannot get a tune out of our heads. The poet shows us how the song won't leave by imitating the maddening repetition all of us feel when this happens to us. Felice Holman does more than tell us, she shows us!

Oftentimes repetition is used as a musical phrase, to help us remember. This is particularly true in ballads that were not written down but passed from singer to singer. Repeating certain lines also emphasizes important actions of the story. Here is the beginning of "Waltzing Matilda."

Once a jolly swagman camped by a billabong
Under the shade of a coolibah tree.
And he sang as he watched and waited till his billy boiled:
"You'll come a-waltzing, Matilda, with me!"

Chorus:
Waltzing, Matilda, waltzing, Matilda,
You'll come a-waltzing, Matilda, with me.
And he sang as he watched and waited till his billy boiled,
"You'll come a-waltzing, Matilda, with me!"

Down came a jumbuck to drink at the billabong,
Up jumped the swagman and grabbed him with glee,
And he sang as he stowed that jumbuck in his tucker
  bag:
"You'll come a-waltzing, Matilda, with me!"

Lines repeated in the same way are called *refrains*, while lines that change a word or two are called *incremental refrains*. Here "You'll come a-waltzing, Matilda, with me" is a refrain, while the lines "And he sang as he watched and waited till his billy boiled" changing to "And he sang as he stowed that jumbuck in his tucker bag" are incremental refrains.

There are many ways you can begin to use repetition. First try using one line that is repeated both at the beginning and the end of a poem. Then write a poem with the same line beginning each stanza. Next think of a phrase that might be worth repeating to your reader, something you want remembered, and use it two or three times. You won't want to use it too many times or it will begin to lose its meaning or become boring.

Always be sure that whatever you choose is worth repeating. If you use an unimportant set of words or phrases that have no real purpose to the meaning of what you are writing, your reader will become weary of hearing the phrase over and over.

Repetition can serve you best as a meaningful way of providing sound and thought patterns where there is no end rhyme. It also lends emphasis to what you wish to say. It can hold a poem together when used well. Used poorly it will make your readers yawn!

ALLITERATION AND ONOMATOPOEIA

Peter Piper picked a peck of pickled pepper;
A peck of pickled pepper Peter Piper picked;
If Peter Piper picked a peck of pickled pepper,
Where's the peck of pickled pepper Peter Piper picked?

It would be difficult to imagine anyone who has not heard this nursery rhyme or tried to say it! I've recently learned that it can be a wonderful cure for the hiccups, if you can say it three times in just one breath! (You might want to try it the next time you have a case of hiccups.)

What you may not know is that this verse is a good example of *alliteration*, the constant repeating of the same letter at the beginning of a succession of words. The same thing happens in this verse:

> Betty Baker bought some butter,
> "But," said she, "this butter's bitter.
> If I put it in my batter,
> It will make my batter bitter."
> So she bought some better butter,
> Butter that was not so bitter,
> Put this butter in her batter,
> Thus she made the batter better.

58

There is something about the sort of alliteration we hear in Peter Piper, Betty Baker, the song "She sells seashells by the seashore," or a circus ringmaster who tells us about "the amazing, astounding antics of the aerial acrobats" that has a touch of humor. Perhaps it is the overuse of the same letter that makes us smile. We become used to using alliteration in our lives, when a house is "spick and span" or the world looks "dark and dreary" or someone seems "hale and hearty." Shel Silverstein's "Sarah Cynthia Sylvia Stout" or "Jimmy Jet" alert us to the possibility of humor in the very alliterative sounds of the name. Jack Prelutsky uses a great deal of alliteration in "The Lurpp Is On The Loose."

> Oh the lurpp is on the loose, the loose,
> the lurpp is on the loose.
> It caused a fretful, frightful fuss
> when it swallowed a ship and ate a bus,
> and now it's after all of us,
> oh the lurpp is on the loose.

Notice the alliterative *l*—lurpp, loose, loose, lurpp, and loose—used five times in the first two lines. In the third line "fretful, frightful fuss" plays on the letters *f* and *l*, and in line 4 "swallowed a ship" is an alliterative use of the *s* (repeated again in the word "bus").

In "Flonster Poem" Jack Prelutsky invents crea-
tures called, respectively, flime, floober, flummie,
fleemie, fleener, floodoo, flink, flibble, flone, floath,
and flakker. In the poem "Four Foolish Ladies" he
writes about "Hattie and Harriet, Hope and Hor-
tense." "Poor Old Penelope" begins

> Poor old Penelope,
> great are her woes,
> a pumpkin has started
> to grow from her nose.
> "My goodness," she warbles,
> "this makes me so glum,
> I'm perfectly certain
> I planted a plum."

Read this aloud to capture the humor that the repeated alliterative sound of the letter *p* creates.

If you are very curious about proper terms, alliteration that begins a word is called *initial alliteration*.
But not all alliteration is humorous, and not all occurs
at the beginning of a word. *Hidden* or *internal alliteration* lurks within words. In the line

> *great are her woes*

we see an example of hidden alliteration, the repetition of the sound of *r* within the words. You can-

not rely on your eyes to tell about hidden alliteration however. You must always *listen* for the sound.

For a further example of alliteration used more seriously, read Tennyson's song on page 69. You may be a long way off from even wanting to try this, because it is difficult. But the more you write, the more you may wish to consider trying this element of sound.

Another element of sound is called *onomatopoeia*. (It took me many years to learn to spell this word without looking in a dictionary!) Onomatopoeia is using words or creating phrases of words that seem to imitate sounds. You can probably think of many of these—bang, hiss, scratch, zoom, ding-dong, crunch, and, of course, the word "buzz."

In her poem "Bandit Bee" Norma Farber writes

> A bee put on a zephyr,
> and wore it as a boot,
> then boldly made
> a bee-line raid
> on banks of honey-loot.

Here Norma Farber is concerned with the idea of a bee, as bandit, looting the flowers for honey. She is not concerned with the sound of bees. In my haiku

Who has the better
right to smell the first summer
rose, bee—you or I?

I am occupied with the idea of my own rights over
the bee's rights, not the sound.
    Edward Lear tells us in a limerick

There was an Old Man in a tree,
Who was horribly bored by a Bee;
    When they said, "Does it buzz?"
    He replied, "Yes, it does!
It's a regular brute of a Bee."

Here the use of the word "buzz" rhyming with "does"
gives somewhat the idea of sound, but Lear's intent
is to be humorous rather than onomatopoetic.
    In his poem "The Bees' Song" Walter de la Mare
writes many lines intent on creating an onomatopoetic sound—that of bees buzzing.

Thousandz of thornz there be
On the Rozez where gozez
The Zebra of Zee . . .

Heavy with blossomz be
The Rozez that growzez
In the thickets of Zee.
Where grazez the Zebra . . .

And he nozez the poziez
Of the Rozez that growzez . . .

Walter de la Mare is building up with his words, with his use of the sound of the letter z, an imitation of the sound of bees.

Alfred, Lord Tennyson in "Come down, O maid" also uses onomatopoeia to create the undercurrent of sound that many bees make in his line

And murmuring of innumerable bees

Another instance of onomatopoeia is found in Eve Merriam's words for the cat on page 77.

You may wish to try using onomatopoeia in a poem that has need for imitation of sound, but onomatopoetic words in themselves are limited. Merely writing the word "buzz" may help a bit, but it is through alliteration, consonance, assonance, metrical rhythms, and even rhyme that the best onomatopoetic sound—or sound of any sort—is created. These types of sounds are discussed in the next chapter.

OFF RHYME, CONSONANCE, AND ASSONANCE

If rhyme is important to you, it is probably because you are becoming aware that it can contribute a great deal to the sound of a poem, giving the idea greater meaning.

What most people think of as rhyme is *end rhyme*, the sounds that agree at the end of the line. We don't know why young children—or even why we— search for rhymes or even make up words (like alone/capone) in order to complete a rhyming sound. We do know that it seems to give us balance and please the ear. Some people believe that rhymes help us to remember a verse or poem. Others feel that rhyme contributes a sort of magic that engages our whole being, a sort of mesmerizing spell weaving words and sound together.

So far we've been concerned with end rhyme (see/me, high/sky, play/day, low/slow, blew/you). These are perfect rhymes, sometimes called complete rhymes, full rhymes, true rhymes, or exact rhymes. You can use any one of these terms.

Sometimes, however, words are used that have

no perfect rhyme. "There is no rhyme for silver," Eve Merriam says in her poem. It is then that we may wish to use what is sometimes called off rhyme but can also be called half rhyme, near rhyme, imperfect rhyme, partial rhyme, or slant rhyme. Any of these terms mean the same.

Off rhyme, used at the end of a line, usually carries the same basic sound. The words have vowels or consonants in common, which the ear accepts as near rhyming. In her poem "Charles" Gwendolyn Brooks writes

> Sick-times, you go inside yourself,
> And scarce can come away.
> You sit and look outside yourself
> At people passing by.

Because Charles is not happy, Gwendolyn Brooks seems to emphasize the feeling by using off rhyme. Certainly she might have found a rhyme for the word *away*. There are many rhyming words that end in the *a* or *ay* sound. But to ask "How does a poem mean?" is to consider that even a choice of an off rhyme reinforces the idea of Charles's "sick-times."

I suggest this because in my poem "Daddy" I decided, because of the sad subject matter, to do this very thing.

only know I loved you
    Daddy
watched you
hoping someday
    maybe
me and you'd
do things real
    crazy
always hoped
you'd call me
    baby—

didn't see
that things were
    shabby
couldn't tell
things went so
    badly
never knew
you were
    unhappy
only knew I loved you
    Daddy

Although *maybe* and *baby* are perfect rhymes, the others (Daddy, crazy, shabby, badly, unhappy) have only the *y* (or *e*) sound in common. The rest of the words express how the speaker feels, but jar against each other much as the speaker is jarred.

William Blake may have done this very thing when he wrote about "The Little Boy Lost."

> "Father! father! where are you going?
> "O do not walk so fast.
> "Speak, father, speak to your little boy,
> "Or else I shall be lost."

Blake was a fine poet and could certainly have found a rhyme for the word *fast* (blast, cast, mast, past or passed, and others). But perhaps he wanted to impress upon his readers the disorientation of a boy being separated from his father.

Perhaps you've noticed that the words *fast* and *lost* have two letters in common, the *st*. When consonants like this agree, not only as end rhymes but in all of our writing, we call this *consonance*.

Emily Dickinson uses off rhyme with consonance in a great many of her poems. She begins "A Narrow Fellow in the Grass" with

> A narrow fellow in the grass
> Occasionally rides;
> You may have met him,—did you not,
> His notice sudden is.

Here the *s* sound is one of consonance. None of the other letters have anything in common. Even the pronunciation or sound of the *i* in *rides* and the sound of *i* in *is* differs. In another poem she writes

> When I have seen the sun emerge
> From his amazing house
> And leave a day at every door,
> A deed in every place . . .

Again we see that because the *c* and the *s* in the words *house* and *place* sound alike, although they are not the same letter, we have a good example of consonance.

Sometimes, however, a rhyme is made by the use of vowel agreement. This was true in "Charles" and "Daddy," where the *y* (pronounced like an *e*) is repeated. Eve Merriam's "Sunset" begins with these lines:

> Yellow and pink as a peach
> left to ripen on the tree

The sound of *e* in *peach* and *tree* forces us to hear this as a rhyme. Rhyme made by the use of vowels is called *assonance*.

Consonance and assonance are used not only for end rhymes but for creating effects in poems. Sometimes they are used together with rhyme to create a totally splendid orchestra of sound. Alfred, Lord

Tennyson uses all sorts of sound patterns in this song:

> The splendor falls on castle walls
> And snowy summits old in story;
> The long light shakes across the lakes,
> And the wild cataract leaps in glory.
> Blow, bugle, blow, set the wild echoes flying,
> Blow, bugle; answer, echoes, dying, dying, dying.
>
> O, hark, O, hear! how thin and clear,
> And thinner, clearer, farther going!
> O, sweet and far from cliff and scar
> The horns of Elfland faintly blowing!
> Blow, let us hear the purple glens replying,
> Blow, bugle; answer, echoes, dying, dying, dying.
>
> O love, they die in yon rich sky,
> They faint on hill or field or river;
> Our echoes roll from soul to soul,
> And grow for ever and for ever.
> Blow, bugle, blow, set the wild echoes flying,
> And answer, echoes, answer, dying, dying, dying.

Tennyson uses not only exact end rhyme in this poem (story/glory, flying/dying, going/blowing, re-plying/dying) but off rhyme as well. In the second stanza lines 1 and 3, you will see consonance in the use of the *r* in *clear* and *scar*. There is a great deal of assonance in the line.

> Blow, bugle, blow, set the wild echoes flying,

where the sound of the long *o* is heard three times.

In addition you will find another use of sound by the repetition used in the last two lines of each stanza. And you will also hear and see that Tennyson uses another form of rhyme, *internal rhyme*, in all three stanzas:

> The splendor falls on castle walls
>
> The long light shakes across the lakes,
>
> O, hark, O, hear! how thin and clear,
>
> O, sweet and far from cliff and scar
>
> O love, they die in yon rich sky,
>
> Our echoes roll from soul to soul,

Notice how *falls* rhymes with *walls*, *shakes* with *lakes*, *hear* with *clear*, *far* with *scar*, *die* with *sky*, and *roll* with *soul*.

As if this were not enough, Tennyson uses yet another sound pattern, that of alliteration. Notice *splendor*, *snowy*, *summits*, and *story* in the first two lines; *long light*, *lakes*, and *leaps* in the next two lines. You may search for other examples if you like!

Shakespeare has used the same kind of internal and end rhyme and alliteration in *Macbeth*.

> Double, double toil and trouble;
> Fire burn and cauldron bubble.

Not only is there end rhyme, *trouble* and *bubble*, but there is internal rhyme, *double* and *trouble*. Notice also the alliteration in *toil* and *trouble*.

Perhaps through looking at these poems and learning more about rhyme and sound (although there is still much I have not told you about), you will begin to understand that there is a great difference between the finest poetry and greeting-card verse. Versifiers (those who write lines that rhyme) do not bother to learn all of the effects of sound, nor the importance of figures of speech (which will be explained in later chapters). When you read poems or verses in anthologies, you will begin to notice how sound and fresh language as well as rhythm contribute to the meaning of a poem.

Meanwhile you can practice using some of these elements in sound. Try writing poems using off rhyme; experiment with consonance and assonance; try writing a few lines using internal rhyme with or without end rhyme. Although it may seem like a great deal to learn, you will begin to understand it with practice.

Rhythm and Metrics

RHYTHM is an important part of our lives. We feel our hearts beat in a steady rhythm. We walk, run, jump rope, and dance in measured pattern. A leaky faucet drips and a telephone rings in rhythm. If these patterns are disturbed, it makes us feel off-balance.

Some people seem to have a better sense of rhythm than others. They are bothered if words do not flow smoothly. Others may have to work harder to sense the beat of a line of poetry. Others never seem to mind if the rhythm is erratic.

Traditionally English poetry was written for many centuries in a measured cadence that we call *meter* or *metrics*. This meter is made up of poetic units called *feet*. The most common of these feet are the *iamb*, the *trochee*, the *anapest*, and the *dactyl*. Learning about these feet enables poets to control the cadence of words, to recognize that meter can help the words to convey a particular mood.

Yet those who never stray from perfect meter are

apt to write singsong verse, the sort of predictable messages we find in greeting cards. What we hope for, in writing our own poetry, is to learn the rules first before we decide to break them for a special effect. Careful craftsmanship honors the feeling we are trying to convey through our words, yet the poet's thoughts should not become crushed under dull attention to metrics at the expense of our real feelings or image. It is a sort of balancing act in which we continually go back to our question *How does a poem mean*?

The *iamb* is the most common foot in English poetry. It is made up of two syllables with a stress, or accent, on the second syllable. A word like *today* and a name like *Marie* are iambic words (today ˘´ Marie ˘´).

Here a short unaccented syllable (˘) is followed by a longer or stressed syllable (´).

Sometimes the entire foot is one word but at other times it is made up of two words, as in the beginning of Valerie Worth's poem "Clock." Notice how we naturally put the accent on the second word:

> Thĭs clóck
> Hăs stópped,
> Sŏme géar
> Ŏr spríng
> Gŏne wróng . . .

Lilian Moore uses the same pattern in the beginning of her poem "While You Were Chasing a Hat."

> The wínd
> that whírled
> your hát
> awáy . . .

Sometimes there will be two iambs in a line. Aileen Fisher's "My Cat and I" begins

> When Í | flóp dówn
> to táke | a rést
> my cát | jumps úp
> upón | my chést.

In "Whistles" Rachel Field uses three iambs:

> Ĭ né|vĕr é|vĕn héar
> The boáts | that páss | bў dáy;
> Bў níght | they seém | sŏ néar,
> Ă-whís|tling dówn | thĕ báy . . .

And Ogden Nash in "Between Birthdays" uses four iambs:

> Mў bírth|dăys táke | sŏ lóng | tŏ stárt
> They cóme | alóng | ă yéar | ăpárt.

The *anapest*, like the iamb, is a rising foot. It has two unaccented or unstressed syllables followed by a stressed syllable and is used in the limerick and humorous verse because it sounds so playful. If you use anapests long enough, your heartbeat will actually speed up!

A word like *disagree* (˘˘´) and a name like *Marianne* (˘˘´) are anapests, but most often it takes two or three words to form an anapestic foot; *in the woods* (˘˘´), *at the door* (˘˘´) are anapestic. Here the accent is put on the last word.

Most everyone will recognize the anapestic beat of Clement Clarke Moore's "A Visit from St. Nicholas."

> 'Twas the night | before Christ|mas,
> when all | through the house
> Not a crea|ture was stir|ring,
> not e|ven a mouse;

In this verse only two anapests are used:

> When he went | to the house,
> And he knocked | on the door—

Shel Silverstein uses three anapests in "The Man in the Iron Pail Mask."

> He's the man | in the i|ron pail mask,
> He can do | the most dif|ficult task . . .

Anapests are most important to know about when you want to write a limerick!

The *trochee* is a falling foot, with the accent on the first syllable followed by an unaccented beat. *Sunny* is a trochaic word (sunny ´˘) and *Richard* (´˘) is a trochaic name. Henry Wadsworth Longfellow's *The Song of Hiawatha* is written entirely in trochees.

> By the | shores of | Gitche | Gumee,
> By the | shining | Big-Sea-|Water,
> Stood the | wigwam | of No|komis,
> Daughter | of the | moon, No|komis . . .

Almost every line of this poem, over 5,600 lines, is written in the meter of the Finnish epic the *Kalevala*, with four trochees to each line (´˘´˘´˘´˘). If you read this poem, it becomes almost like a drumbeat in your head. Other poets employ the trochee in smaller doses. David McCord tells about "Marty's Party" with two trochees in a line.

> Marty's | party?
> Jamie | came. He
> seemed to | Judy
> dreadful | rude. He
> joggled | Davy,
> spilled his | gravy,
> squeezed a | melon
> seed at | Helen . . .

X. J. Kennedy uses trochaic patterns in many of his poems in *Brats.*

Pláying | sóccer, | Pláto | Fóley
Kícked a | wásp's nest | pást the | góalie.
Sóon the | whóle crowd | júmped up | róaring
Whén those | wínged things | stárted | scóring.

Eve Merriam uses trochees to begin her poem "Aelourophobe"—a good word for someone who has a morbid fear of cats. With its accent on the first beat, the trochee seems to mimic the adjectives she finds for cats.

Tóm or | tábby
snárling | grábby
hísser | póuncer
flóuter | flóuncer

Another falling foot is the *dactyl. Elephant* (′ ˘ ˘) is a dactylic word; *Jennifer* is a dactylic name (′ ˘ ˘). Notice how we accent the first syllable of both words as we read or speak and leave the last two syllables unstressed.

It is unlikely that you would ever write a poem entirely in dactyls. Longfellow used it in "Evangeline."

Thís ĭs thĕ | fŏrest prĭ|mḗvăl. Thĕ | múrmŭrĭng
| pínĕs ănd thĕ | hémlŏcks
Beárdĕd wĭth | mŏss, ănd ĭn | gármĕnts | grḗen,
ĭndís|tínct ĭn thĕ | twílĭght . . .

Here the dactyls sound heavy and ponderous and are usually combined with the trochee, as in Robert Louis Stevenson's "Nest Eggs."

Bírds ăll thĕ | súnnÿ dăy
Flúttĕr ănd | quárrĕl
Hére ĭn thĕ | árbŏur-líke
Ténd ŏf thĕ | láurĕl.

Stevenson uses both trochee and dactyl to create a feeling of urgency and speed in "From a Railway Carriage."

Fástĕr thăn | fáiriĕs, | fástĕr thăn | wítchĕs,
Brídgĕs ănd | hóusĕs, | hédgĕs ănd | dítchĕs . . .

A sense of mystery pervades Christina Rossetti's "Goblin Market" as she weaves dactyls and trochees together in varying combinations:

Mórning and | évening
Maíds heárd the | góblins cry
"Cóme búy our | órchard fruíts,
Cóme búy, | cóme búy:
Ápples and | quínces,
Lémons and | óranges
Plúmp únpecked | chérries,
Mélons and | ráspberries . . .

As you begin to learn about metrical feet, it is good to remember that the rising feet, the iamb and the anapest, go well together, as do the falling feet, the trochee and the dactyl. If you have heard a verse that doesn't "sound right," it is usually because the writer has been careless in putting the feet together!

Of course you can write poetry without learning metrics, but people who do learn about them always find that the patterns they create add a great deal to the feeling and mood of their poems. And then they want to go on and learn about all the other feet!

Figures of Speech

ONE OF THE differences between pleasant verse and fine poetry is the way in which the poet, unlike the writer of greeting cards, uses *figures of speech*.

In rhymed verse, the sentiments we buy or may even write ourselves to honor someone on a birthday, we are concerned with meter and rhyme and message. We seldom think about other elements. The rhyme itself usually has a singsong quality. It is always perfect, not straying from the beat. It expresses a sentiment such as "I like you" or "I miss you" or "Happy Birthday" or "Get Well." That is its purpose.

The purpose of poetry is not to give a message, but to ask the reader to discover how the poem may be meaningful. We do not *tell* in poetry; we *show*. The image we give to our readers should help them to understand what we are speaking about.

80

We do not have to say "I love you" because we are arranging our words and rhythms and picture to give the feeling of love.

Using *figures of speech*, sometimes called *figurative language*, is one way to write better poems. There are many such figures, some very complicated and too difficult to attempt when you are first beginning to write.

The figures here, *simile*, *metaphor*, and *personification*, are among the most well-known. They are the sort of figurative language the oldest of primitive peoples and the youngest of children use all the time. They offer many possibilities of expression for all of us.

THE SIMILE

The *simile* is a figure of speech that compares one thing to another using the introductory words *like* or *as*. We use similes in our speech every day. We say that someone is "quiet as a mouse" or "crazy like a fox" but these similes have become clichés. The poet's challenge is to see or hear things in a new way, to offer fresh comparisons of things that may have gone unnoticed.

In her poem "Ladybug" Charlotte Zolotow makes this observation:

> Little ladybug,
> with your
> glazed red wings
> and small black polka dots,
> you look
> like a
> porcelain statue
> until
> suddenly
> you
> fly
>   away.

Perhaps Charlotte Zolotow once looked at a lady-bug and thought, "It looks like a porcelain statue" and then wrote this. Or perhaps she wrote the idea down to use in a poem, or carried it about in her head until it was bursting to be written as a simile.

Perhaps Judith Thurman observed birds settled on telephone wires before she wrote her poem "New Notebook." Or did she write in a new notebook and think about crows on telephone lines?

> Lines
> in a new notebook
> run, even and fine,
> like telephone wires
> across a snowy landscape.
>
> With wet, black strokes
> the alphabet settles between them,
> comfortable as a flock of crows.

The first simile occurs when she compares the lines to telephone wires; the second, when she says the alphabet settles "comfortable as a flock of crows."

Tsumori Kunimoto uses simile in his poem about wild geese.

The wild geese returning
Through the misty sky—
Behold they look like
A letter written
In faded ink!

   Sometimes listening carefully helps us to become aware of sounds that are alike. X. J. Kennedy writes in "Flying Uptown Backwards"

Squeezing round a bend, train shrieks
Like chalk on gritty blackboards.

People talk or read or stare.
Street names pass like flashcards.

Hope this train keeps going on
Flying uptown backwards.

Here one simile compares two sounds, the train shrieking like squeaky chalk. The other is a visual simile where X. J. Kennedy tells us that on a train the names of streets go by "like flashcards."
   In her poem "Frog" Valerie Worth uses three similes.

The spotted frog
Sits quite still
On a wet stone;

He is green
With a luster
Of water on his skin;

His back is mossy
With spots, and green
Like moss on a stone;

His gold-circled eyes
Stare hard
Like bright metal rings;

When he leaps
He is like a stone
Thrown into the pond;

Water rings spread
After him, bright circles
Of green, circles of gold.

Have you ever noticed a frog's back to be mossy, with spots and green "Like moss on a stone"? Have you ever thought of a frog's eyes "Like bright metal rings"? Have you watched a frog leap into the water "like a stone/Thrown into the pond"? The poet has observed carefully to make her comparisons—her similes.

At one school where I taught, a huge bed of calla lilies grew each Spring. All of us would go out to observe them, to note what these tall white lilies reminded us of, and to write about them. One year we put up a giant display for Open House and called it "426 Ways to Look at a Calla Lily." Among the poems were many using similes, for this flower seemed to look like an old-fashioned telephone, like a ballerina's skirt, like a dust mop, like a slide for a snail. But if the children had not spent a lot of time and looked carefully, these similarities might never have been noticed.

It takes time to look around you. Watch the clouds, how they seem to be shapes of animals or castles. Look at bushes, at trees, and notice what else they might be. Using the words *like*, *as*, or *as though*, you may create some similes that can be used in the poems you write.

METAPHOR

Power lines have always fascinated me. Once I rode through the French countryside observing miles and miles of power lines, which, because of their odd shape and wires, looked like cats with long whiskers. (I even drew pictures of them in my journal.) No matter where I go, I seem to find that the intricate structure of power lines suggests something new to me. Sometimes they are animals, sometimes people with heads, bodies, arms, and hands that reach out to other power lines.

One day driving home from the Los Angeles airport, I noticed a row of power lines and jotted down a few notes about them. At home I wrote my poem "Power Lines."

> Thin robots,
> Spun of wire lace,
> Plant their feet down
> Each in one place.
>
> Standing tall
> In a measured row,
> Watching over
> Highways below.

87

Holding hands
With steel strand rope,
Gray, faceless.
No fear. No hope.

This poem is a *metaphor*, for it says that one thing (power lines) is something else (thin robots). If I had written that a power line is *like* a robot, I would have created a simile. If I had said that a power line stands tall *as* a mountain, I would have written a simile. But I did not. I said that power lines *are* robots and told about their feet, their height, their hands, their heads without faces, and something about their lack of feelings.

Closely related to the simile, a metaphor makes a comparison by telling us that one thing *is* another so well that we are able to imagine both things to be linked. If a metaphor is fresh, we can see something new and unusual—something we might never have seen before.

One of the ways to tell the difference between a simile and a metaphor is by the use of the introductory or connecting words. A simile uses the words *like*, *as*, or *though*. A metaphor usually uses some part of the verb to be, usually the word *is*. Sometimes as in "Power Lines" the title suggests the comparison or metaphor to follow. Wallace Stevens does this in his poem "The Brave Man."

The sun, that brave man,
Comes through boughs that lie in wait,
That brave man.

Green and gloomy eyes
In dark forms of the grass
Run away.

The good stars,
Pale helms and spiky spurs,
Run away.

Fears of my bed,
Fears of life and fears of death,
Run away.

That brave man comes up
From below and walks without meditation,
That brave man.

In her book *The Sun is a Golden Earring* Natalia
Belting uses many metaphors. The title itself is a
metaphor—the sun *is* a golden earring. If you can
imagine the sun as an earring, you will find this a
good metaphor. If not, you might like it when she
writes "The Wind is a man with a spade in his hand."
Or you might agree with this metaphor:

Once, when the sky was very near the earth
a woman hoeing in her garden took off her necklace
and hung it in the sky.
The stars are her silver necklace.

Metaphors, if they are good, have a strange power to help us see our world in a new perspective. While we may not respond to someone who lectures us with warnings or good advice about how things are or will be, we relate immediately to excellent images. Like the ancient peoples who first expressed themselves in metaphor, we understand immediately what is meant by the "foot of a mountain" or "the mouth of a river."

Suppose someone told you

> Hold fast to dreams
> For if dreams die
> It's going to be hard for you
> To get by.
>
> Hold fast to dreams
> For when dreams go
> You can be disappointed
> You know.

Would you listen or be interested? Probably not. But, by using metaphor, Langston Hughes tells us in "Dreams"

> Hold fast to dreams
> For if dreams die
> Life is a broken-winged bird
> That cannot fly.

Hold fast to dreams
For if dreams go
Life is a barren field
Frozen with snow.

Introduced to such vivid pictures as "a broken-winged bird" and "a barren field/Frozen with snow," we can make the connection and really understand more fully. The poet enables us to see in a way that goes beyond a concept that is dull and without much meaning.

Metaphors arouse our feelings and our imaginations. They may appear to be strange, for they lift us out of reality. We know, for example, that life is not *really* a broken-winged bird or a frozen field. But these comparisons arrest our senses. They create something beyond reality that brings us, oddly enough, to see reality very clearly.

When Norma Farber writes that "Marbles that grow on trees—mostly are cherries" we are surprised. We know that marbles do not, in our world, grow on trees. Yet we see a fresh image that allows our imaginations to soar!

The metaphors in Valerie Worth's "Sun" are a constant delight.

The sun
Is a leaping fire
Too hot
To go near,

But it will still
Lie down
In warm yellow squares
On the floor

Like a flat
Quilt, where
The cat can curl
And purr.

We know, of course, that the sun is a star, a maelstrom of hot gases, but what happens to us when we are told that it can also be seen as a warm quilt?

When you are reading poetry, you may find that metaphors are more difficult to spot than similes. Sometimes the poet gives us a clue and sometimes not. In this poem "From the Japanese" Eve Merriam writes

The summer night
is a dark blue hammock
slung between the white pillars of day.

I lie there
cooling myself
with the straw-colored
flat round fan
of the full moon.

We can recognize in the first stanza the metaphor that tells us that the summer night "is a dark blue hammock." But in the second stanza there is no connective word; the poet merely implies that the full moon is a "flat round fan." She expects us, as intelligent readers, to make the connection.

In her poem "Safety Pin" Valerie Worth writes

> Closed, it sleeps
> On its side
> Quietly,
> The silver
> Image
> Of some
> Small fish. . . .

Again, the poet expects us to make the comparison of a closed safety pin to a small, silver fish.

Sometimes long metaphors include the use of connective words such as *like* and *as if* so that at first we may mistake the poem for a series of similes. We must therefore read the entire poem to understand whether it is a metaphor or simile. "The Hills" by Rachel Field is such a poem.

> Sometimes I think the hills
> That loom across the harbor
> Lie there like sleeping dragons,

Crouched one above another,
With trees for tufts of fur
Growing all up and down
The ridges and humps of their backs,
And orange cliffs for claws
Dipped in the sea below.
Sometimes a wisp of smoke
Rises out of the hollows
As if in their dragon sleep
They dreamed of strange old battles.

What if the hills should stir
Some day and stretch themselves,
Shake off the clinging trees
And all the clustered houses?

Have you ever imagined hills as dragons or clouds as castles? Have you seen a tree trunk that seemed to have a strange face outlined in its bark? Do you ever watch shadows and pretend they are beasts? All of these—and more—have the possibility for metaphoric poems.

For me, the finest poems are those that use metaphor well, because they enable us to see, for the first time, images we might never have imagined for ourselves. Once seen, they become a part of us, enriching our perceptions and our lives.

PERSONIFICATION

When Joan Aiken writes

> There was a young lady of Newington Green
> Had the luck to be loved by a sewing machine
> Its foot was so slender, its eye was so bright
> It sewed so obligingly, morning or night
> On nylon or seersucker, silk or sateen
> Her sturdy, reliable Singer machine!

she is using *personification*, a figure of speech that assigns human qualities to something that does not, in reality, have these characteristics. "The Ballad of Newington Green" tells of a sturdy, reliable sewing machine with a bright eye, a slender foot, and love for the young lady. While we know that sewing machines can be reliable and sturdy, that the needle might be called the eye or the treadle the foot, the idea of a sewing machine who "loves" goes beyond the characteristics we would normally think of in a sewing machine.

You may remember, when you were very small, thinking that the moon (especially when you rode in a bus or car at night) was following you. Young children often believe that everything is endowed with the same sort of life they have. They scold their milk for spilling, or shout to their bicycles not to roll away. Poets never seem to lose this ability to give life to inanimate objects. Long after they have put their teddy bears away or learned that the sun is a huge star, they assign to these things a quality of animation that makes them seem alive.

In her poem "Foghorns" Lilian Moore writes

> The foghorns moaned
>   in the bay last night
> so sad
> so deep
> I thought I heard the city
>   crying in its sleep.

If you've heard foghorns, you know that they make a very plaintive sad sound. To Lilian Moore this sounded like the same moan that people make. By transferring the "moan" of the person to a foghorn, she personifies a foghorn. In addition, she adds to this idea by having the city "cry"—as if in response to the moan of foghorns. It is true that a city cannot cry nor a foghorn moan, but this sort of personification gives us a much stronger picture of the sadness of the foghorns' sound.

In this poem about "The Wind" James Stephens says

> The wind stood up, and gave a shout;
> He whistled on his fingers, and
>
> Kicked the withered leaves about,
> And thumped the branches with his hand,
>
> And said he'd kill, and kill, and kill;
> And so he will! And so he will!

Here the poet conceives of the wind as someone who can not only make loud noises, whistle, kick leaves about, and thump branches, but promises to wreak a lot of destruction. By using personification, he forces us to think of the sort of person who indulges in such acts. James Stephens's picture of the wind is far more striking than if he had only said that the wind whistles, whirls leaves, moves the branches of trees, and raises a lot of havoc.

In "I Took a Little Stick" Elizabeth Coatsworth personifies Spring.

> Spring tried and tried, but could not make
> The water run beneath the snow,
> I took a little stick and scratched
> A way for it to go.

It curved into a waterfall
(I cleared the drain, so it might sing)—
Oh, I've been busy half the day
Just helping Spring.

This is a simple form of personification, just showing one quality of Spring, its perseverance, how it "tried and tried." But it also presents Spring as a person, helped by the writer.

In a book called *A Circle of Seasons* I enjoyed personifying all the seasons. I wrote about Spring.

Spring brings out her baseball bat, swings it through
   the air,
Pitches bulbs and apple blossoms, throws them where
   it's bare,
Catches dogtooth violets, slides to meadowsweet,
Bunts a breeze and tags the trees with green buds
   everywhere.

This is part of the Winter personification:

Winter etches windowpanes, fingerpaints in white,
Sculptures strange soft shapes of snow that glisten in
   the night,
Filigrees the snowflake, spins icicles of glass,
Paints the ground in hoarfrost, its needles sharp with
   light.

To Spring I gave all the attributes of a baseball player who swings, pitches, throws, catches, slides, bunts, and tags. Winter is personified as an artist who etches, fingerpaints, sculptures, and paints.

Personification can be very simple. It can be a foghorn that moans or a city that cries, or it can become more complicated as in the example of the wind.

It is probably best to keep your first attempt at personification simple. Think for a moment of how you might personify the sun. What would it do that you, or someone you know, can do? Think about stars. Could they turn themselves on? In a poem called "Taking Turns" Norma Farber writes

> When sun goes home
> behind the trees,
> and locks her shutters tight—
>
> then stars come out
> with silver keys
> to open up the night.

Here the personification of both sun and stars together gives us a picture of what we ourselves do when night comes. We go home and lock up our houses or even open our door with a key.

You might like to try personifying some holiday, as Felice Holman does in

THE YEAR

goes
skidding
down
to
the
bottom
of the
cal-
en-
dar
slip-
ping
out   HAPPY NEW YEAR!
the   top
end.   the
Then   to
ZOOM   Up

If a year skids, slips, and zooms, think what April Fool's Day or the Fourth of July might do. What verbs or actions could you use for your personification?

Personification is often used as a part of metaphor. Read "The Brave Man" on page 89 to find out what human characteristics Wallace Stevens assigns to the sun.

Personification is a figure of speech we can't use in all of the poems we write, but when used well it adds immeasurably to the freshness of a poem, helping us to imaginative flights of fancy!

Other Forms

IF YOU SAT DOWN to your dinner table every evening and were always offered the same food, you would probably become very tired of that food. If you had only one shirt to wear, you would probably begin to want a different color, a different style. We look for variety in almost everything we do.

For a long time I wrote poetry in the same way, using couplets, tercets, quatrains, and combinations of these rhyming patterns. It took me a long time to realize that there might be other forms for my writing. When I began to discover the possibility of using syllabic patterns, especially the haiku and cinquain, and explored arranging words into shapes, I had not broken from tradition, but had added other ways to express myself.

But choice also brings decision making. How do I know what form to use?

Oftentimes I don't. I will start with one idea in a

certain form and realize that the poem isn't working. So I choose another, and sometimes three or four, before I decide which form is helping, or working against, my observations and ideas.

Somewhere, in reading about the cinquain, haiku, limerick, ballad, open form, or concrete poem, I know you will find a form you'll want to try, one to best express your feelings. And you'll come to learn that a funny story can't be told well in a cinquain, nor a serious observation do very well in a limerick.

One of the most difficult things about writing a poem is finding the right form. At least that is true for me. One of my students once decided to write a poem about television. He tried couplets, tercets, quatrains, a ballad, a haiku, a cinquain, free verse, a shape poem, and even more. Some worked out very well. Others were all wrong. But in trying and practicing, he learned a great deal about patterns and forms. And that is really the point, isn't it?

HAIKU

Well! Hello down there,
friend snail! When did you arrive
in such a hurry?

Issa

Most of you will recognize that this short poem, written in just seventeen syllables, is a *haiku*. Haiku has been written in Japan for centuries but has become popular as a form for classroom writing in the United States during the past twenty-five years. Unfortunately, haiku is not an "easy" kind of poem to write, as some people believe.

The first thing to know is that the word "hai-ku" itself means "beginning phrase." Haiku was originally the beginning of a much longer poem that developed from seventeen syllables.

Today haiku is considered a complete form in itself with rules not only for the subject matter but for creating the sort of picture into which readers can put themselves. The form is strict. I have seen haiku translated from the Japanese in four lines, but the form used most often is three lines. The first line has five syllables, the second seven, and the third five—a total of seventeen.

One important rule concerns the subject matter. The poem must always refer to something in nature or use what is called a "season word." Much of the haiku that has been translated from the Japanese uses the nature symbols of Japan. But because we live in the United States, it is better to use symbols of seasons where we live. For example, if you have visited Japan, you will know that cherry blossoms signify spring. Other flowers and plants may symbolize spring where you live, such as crocus or skunk cabbage. In my garden spring comes with Oriental magnolias, daffodils, and stock.

You may always use the words "Spring," "Summer," "Autumn" or "Fall," and "Winter," but season words are even more interesting. For example, if you were describing something that happened in fall, you might consider the word "football" or "the beginning of school."

Basho, one of the great haiku writers of the seventeenth century, wrote

> A dry leaf drifting
> down to earth clings to a strange
> green-spotted mushroom.

We know that it is fall because this is the season when leaves become dry.

Anyone the world over might recognize the season word for summer in this haiku, also by Basho.

> The best I have to
> offer you is the small size
> of the mosquitoes.

Here is one by Issa, one of my favorite haiku poets.

> What a pretty kite
> the beggar's children fly high
> above their hovel!

Here, as in Japan, we recognize kite flying to be a spring activity. And for winter a Japanese-American haiku poet, Kazue Mizumura, writes

> A lonely sparrow
> Hops upon the snow and prints
> Sets of maple leaves.

You may notice that in all of the haiku, the poet writes about only one thing—a dry leaf, mosquitoes, a kite, and a sparrow. Instead of trying to describe many many things about each season, a haiku concentrates on just one thing. This thing must seem to be happening just at the moment we read about it, as though the poets were pointing out something they wished you to see. Notice how the *present tense* is always used in a haiku. *One thing, happening now!*

It is possible that you may wish to write a haiku from memory, remembering something you saw. Still you should pretend it is happening at this very moment—as though you are calling to someone to come and watch it happen.

Haiku should also present a picture of something you want your reader to think about further, a sort of beginning for your own imaginative pictures. Can you see the dry leaf drifting down? What does the strange green-spotted mushroom look like? Can you picture the mosquitoes, someone offering you a look at these tiny insects? Can you watch the kite sailing off above the hovel of the beggar's children? And do you follow the way the lonely sparrow prints sets of maple leaves with his feet?

One of my favorite haikus by Joso says

> That duck, bobbing up
> from the green deeps of a pond,
> has seen something strange. . . .

This makes me wonder what strange thing the duck has seen; my mind goes down to the bottom of the pond and searches about.

Here is one of the most famous of all Bashos haikus:

> An old silent pond . . .
> A frog jumps into the pond,
>   splash! Silence again.

Imagine you are watching a frog jump into a silent pond, hearing the splash, and then listening for the silence again. You may further imagine the circles of water, the ripples made by the frog, how they begin and then cease. Another haiku, by Chosu, says

> Broken and broken
> again on the sea, the moon
>   so easily mends.

Can you imagine watching the moon's reflection on waves, whole and broken, whole and broken, creating an image that repeats itself over and over?

One haiku I like to share with my students enables all of us to appreciate how amazingly a haiku, made up of only seventeen syllables, can give us a picture in a few words. Written by Issa, it says

> If things were better
> for me, flies, I'd invite you
>   to share my supper.

What does this tell you? Do you see a king sitting at a banquet table brushing away the flies? What sort of person is speaking? The words "If things were better for me" give us a clue. This person would like to share some food with the flies, but apparently things are so bad that the tiniest crumb cannot be spared. The picture then must be of someone who is poor. Each of us will see something different in these words. It might be a child, a boy, a girl, a man, or a woman. Who is this person? Why is he or she poor? How does he or she speak to the flies—in a sad or complaining voice? Or is it a voice of humor? Where is this person sitting? In a small room or outside? Do you think of someone who is mean, or are the words filled with kindness and concern for the fly? And have you noticed that the season word "flies" lets us know it is summer?

Imagine being able to say all this in just fourteen words—seventeen syllables. If we were to write it in prose, we might have to say something like: "One summer there was a poor person who had so little to eat that when flies came around he apologized to them for not sharing supper." None of these words convey the same feeling as is found in the seventeen-syllable haiku.

Haiku helps us to use words well, to make each word count. You will notice that words are not repeated in a haiku. There must be a good reason for each word. You may also have noticed that a haiku does not use rhyme.

Writing haiku is not easy. It is really the hardest kind of poem that I know of to write well. But in haiku are many reminders for all kinds of writing: to observe things happening and to write about them, to invite your reader to share what you have seen, to learn to use words well, wasting none of them, and to make of your poetry, whatever form it takes, not a long recital of many things, but of one thing, keenly observed and felt.

THE CINQUAIN

The *cinquain*, one of my favorite forms, is a five-line poem. If you know French, you'll know that *cinq* is the word for "five." There are two syllables in the first line, four in the second, six in the third, eight in the fourth, and two in the fifth.

— —

— — — —

— — — — — —

— — — — — — — —

— —

The cinquain was developed by Adelaide Crapsey, who studied metrical forms and probably took some of her ideas from the three-line, seventeen-syllable haiku. But the cinquain is not like the haiku. It does not have the stringent rules, the necessity for a subject in nature, the present tense, or the need for a season-word. Like the haiku, however, it uses no rhyme.

Chances are you've been in a classroom where cinquain is written. But you may have to change some of your ideas! What many English teachers teach is a language-arts cinquain, which sometimes counts words rather than syllables and is nothing more than an exercise in identifying and writing nouns, verbs, adjectives, a sentence, a synonym, and/or an antonym. It has many variations.

The true cinquain is a form in which we are not concerned with parts of speech; rather we try to express ourselves in some image or thought, using one or perhaps even two sentences. The twenty-two-syllable pattern is just long enough to allow us room for our poem, yet helps us to be succinct, not to waste any words.

In "The Warning" Adelaide Crapsey wrote

> Just now
> Out of the strange
> Still dusk . . . as strange, as still . . .
> A white moth flew. Why am I grown
> So cold?

This cinquain expresses her feelings about seeing a moth at night and the fears it arouses in her. "Niag-ara" describes the falls.

> How frail
> Above the bulk
> Of crashing water hangs,
> Autumnal, evanescent, wan,
> The moon.

In the first poem she has used two sentences, and in the second only one.

You might like to compare Adelaide Crapsey's cinquain about "Winter" to one written in a language-arts class.

> The cold
> With steely clutch
> Grips all the land . . . alack,
> The little people in the hills
> Will die!

Think about how a poet views winter with its "steely clutch." Now read this one:

> Winter,
> cool, cold, chill, raw,
> shivering, shuddering,
> Winter is a very cold time.
> White time.

While the student has listed in order a noun, adjectives, verbs, a statement, and a synonym, there is nothing said here that is new. In Crapsey's cinquain we are given a "steely clutch" and a thought about what will happen to the people in the hills. In the student's cinquain we simply hear a list of words and one commonplace thought.

A cinquain, like all good poetry, should describe in a fresh way. The first cinquain I wrote, "little o," happened because of a television program I was watching, showing a picture of our planet in space.

> little
> o, the earth, bathed
> in ocean, how bravely
> you tumble through the black nothing
> of space

Another day I was looking at my daughter who came in from a camping trip and wrote

> T-shirt,
> you're my best thing
> though you've faded so much
> no one knows what you said when you
> were new.

In the cinquain you may not split syllables from line to line. For example, if you are writing about an astronaut, you cannot begin

> Astro-
> naut

Astronaut is a three-syllable word, so it must be used on the second, third, or fourth line as the diagram shows.

1. ___ ___
2. As tro naut ___
   ___ As tro naut
3. As tro naut ___ ___ ___
   ___ as tro naut ___ ___
   ___ ___ as tro naut ___
   ___ ___ ___ as tro naut
4. As tro naut ___ ___ ___ ___
   ___ as tro naut ___ ___ ___
   ___ ___ as tro naut ___ ___
   ___ ___ ___ as tro naut ___
   ___ ___ ___ ___ as tro naut ___
   ___ ___ ___ ___ ___ as tro naut
5. ___ ___

Your cinquain might begin

> When an
> astronaut leaves

or

> If a
> brave astronaut

or

> I watched
> a moon landing
> when an astronaut came

Cinquains may actually strike you as some sort of mathematical puzzle—how to put the words you wish to say into the right order, while paying attention to the form. This is part of the fun of writing them—moving words about while maintaining the sense of what is said.

Try writing a cinquain and see how it works for you. Some of my students find it a splendid way to express a brief thought or show a striking image. If you try again and again and don't enjoy it, move on to another form. Not everyone likes the cinquain as much as I do.

THE LIMERICK

Limericks are not only delightful to read, but perhaps even more fun when you can write them yourself. Once you've practiced anapestic lines and know the difference between an iamb ($\smile\acute{}$) and an anapest ($\smile\smile\acute{}$), you'll have no difficulty composing a lot of them.

The limerick, however, does have rules. And people who write them without knowing the rules may come up with a funny idea, but often fail to carry it through because they don't observe the metrical rules of making certain that the anapestic pattern is always there. It's sort of a mathematical exercise in part, but even more important is the notion that because the anapest is a lighthearted foot, the rhythm helps to carry the lighthearted idea.

Here's how it works. First, the limerick is a five-line poem.

> There was once a young fellow of Wall
> Who grew up so amazingly tall
>   That his friends dug a pit
>   Where he'd happily sit
> When he wished to converse with them all.

You will notice that lines 1, 2, and 5 always rhyme with each other. Lines 3 and 4 also rhyme with each other. So a limerick is built upon two rhyme sounds.

Lines 1, 2, and 5 all have three feet. Lines 3 and 4 both have 2 feet. In this limerick each foot is anapestic, with three in the first line, three in the second line, two in the third line, two in the fourth line, and three in the fifth line. It's important to learn these rules, and then learn that there can be exceptions.

The exceptions are that we can always substitute an iamb for the *first foot in any line*. For example, instead of saying

> Thĕre wăs onće | ă yŏung fél|lŏw ŏf Wáll

we could say

> Thĕre wás | ă yŏung fél|lŏw ŏf Wáll.

We could also change the second line from

> Whŏ grĕw úp | sŏ ămáz|ĭnglў táll

to read

> Whŏ grĕw | sŏ ămáz|ĭnglў táll.

Here we are keeping the last two anapests and only changing the first. The rhythm is not appreciably affected.

In the third line we could change from

That hĭs frié̆nds | dŭg ă pít

to

Hĭs frié̆nds | dŭg ă pít

and change the fourth line

Whĕre he̎'d háp|pĭlÿ sít

to

Ănd urged | hĭm tŏ sít

and the fifth line from

Whĕn he̎ wished | tŏ cŏnvérse | wĭth thĕm áll

to

Tŏ talk | ănd cŏnvérse | wĭth thĕm áll.

Our changed limerick now reads

> There was a young fellow of Wall
> Who grew so amazingly tall
> His friends dug a pit
> And urged him to sit
> To talk and converse with them all.

There is nothing wrong with this limerick except that taking away the anapests in the beginning and substituting iambs for the anapests helps to kill the happy rhythm. It seems less humorous.

Suppose we decide to abandon *all* anapests. Here is how it might look and sound:

> There was a boy of Wall   ˘ ´ | ˘ ´ | ˘ ´
> Who grew to be so tall   ˘ ´ | ˘ ´ | ˘ ´
> He made a pit   ˘ ´ | ˘ ´ |
> Where he could sit   ˘ ´ | ˘ ´
> Below and talk to all.   ˘ ´ | ˘ ´ | ˘ ´

Obviously, this is no longer a good poem and certainly is not a limerick. It is just a verse written in iambs.

A limerick does not always use thirteen anapests, but it does retain the rhythm by making sure that the second foot and third foot of each line is an anapest. Here is how that works:

> There was *ăn ŏld mán | frŏm Blăckhéath*
> Who sat *ŏn hĭs sét | ŏf fălse teéth*.

"Oh dear, *bless my heart*,"
He said, *with a start*,
"I've bit*ten myself* | *underneath*."

You can see quickly that in this example by an un-
known author every line begins with an iamb but
is followed with anapests.
Here's another:

There was a young woman named Bright,
*Who tra*veled much faster than light,
She set off one day
*In a re*lative way
And returned on the previous night.

In this limerick, also written by an anonymous au-
thor, the first three lines each begin with an iamb.
The last two are all anapestic. In *Pigericks* Arnold
Lobel writes

There was a wet pig from Fort Wayne
*Who was sud*denly caught in the rain.
*His suspen*ders and belt
Were the sort that would melt,
*So his trou*sers were swept down the drain.

Here only the first line begins with an iamb.
  This anonymous limerick reads

*Ăn épi*cure, dining at Crewe,
Foŭnd qúite a large mouse in his stew.
   *Săid the wái*ter, "Don't shout
   Ănd wáve it about
Ŏr the rést will be wanting one too."

Notice that lines, 1, 2, and 4 begin with iambs, while lines 3 and 5 begin with anapests.

  Or read aloud this one by Gelett Burgess:

Ĭ wísh that my room had a floor.
Ĭ dón't so much care for a door.
   *Bŭt thĭs wálk*ing around
   *Wĭthoŭt toúch*ing the ground
*Ĭs gét*ting to be quite a bore.

Here lines 1, 2, and 5 begin with iambs. The others are anapestic.

  By now you know that you can begin any line with an iamb *or* an anapest, in any combination of beginnings. But there are several more exceptions. One concerns the last foot, which must always begin with an anapest but can add another unstressed beat for the rhyming effect.

There was a young wo*măn frŏm Nígĕr*
Who rode on the back *ŏf ă tígĕr*.
   They returned *frŏm the ríde*
   With the la*dy ĭnsíde*
And a smile on the face *ŏf the tígĕr*.

Here you will see that the extra syllable (*ger*) in lines 1, 2, and 5 may be added, but the beginning of the foot must have an anapestic rhythm.

There was a young wom̆an frŏm Nígĕr

You could even write

There was a young girl ŏf Thĕrmópy̆lăe

because you would be keeping the anapestic rhythm, only adding two extra beats. (And, of course, you'd have to find a rhyming word or set of words for Thermopylae!)

There is one other exception to the rules about a limerick. The first limerick writer we know of, Edward Lear, often repeated a rhyming word.

> There was an old man with a beard
> Who said, "It is just as I feared.
>   Two owls and a wren,
>   Four larks and a hen
> Have all made their nest in my beard."

or

> There was an Old Man who said, "Well!
> Will *nobody* answer this bell?

I have pulled day and night
Till my hair has grown white.
But nobody answers this bell!"

or

There was an Old Person of Bangor,
Whose face was distorted with anger;
He tore off his boots
And subsisted on roots,
That borascible Person of Bangor.

Most limericks do not use this repeating pattern, but it might be a way for you to begin, especially if you are using a difficult word like "Bangor." On the other hand, you might search for another rhyme, like "hang her" or "rang her," if the sense would happen to fit.

If all of these rules and exceptions have made you dizzy, let's recap them.

1. A limerick is made up of two metrical feet, the iamb and the anapest.
2. The iamb may be used only as the starting foot, never in the middle and never at the end.
3. Lines 1, 2, and 5 have three feet and rhyme.
4. Lines 3 and 4 have two feet and rhyme.
5. Anapests must always be used in the second and third feet of lines 1, 2, and 5. Anapests must always be used as the second feet in lines 3 and 4.

6. In some cases, an additional beat or two beats may be added to the third foot in lines 1, 2, and 5.

To help you further, always read your lines aloud. With practice you'll soon be able to hear if the limerick doesn't romp along.

One wonderful thing about writing a limerick is that you can use your imagination not only to make up names but to think of humorous situations. A limerick is not a serious kind of a poem—indeed, the funnier you can make it, the better!

FREE VERSE AND OPEN FORMS

Not long ago I was visiting a class and asked students if they ever wrote poetry. One boy volunteered that he wrote poetry all the time. "What kind do you write?" I asked, thinking he might tell me whether his work was serious or funny. "Oh," he answered, "I just write down whatever I think. I like to be creative."

Later, when I saw his poems, I realized that his idea of poetry was simply to write prose and arrange it in lines. Some people would call this *free verse* or *open form*. I see a great deal of so-called poems written this way, by students and adults. By "free verse" they seem to mean that poetry is nothing more than what John Ciardi calls a "spillage of raw emotion"—some thought put down any old way, without rhyme or even much reason.

What I think we should mean by free verse, or open form, is that which does not make itself a slave to rhyme or traditional metrical patterns. It becomes *free* of any restricting rules and remains open-minded, if you like, to new sorts of patterns. Most poets who write this way may have abandoned traditional couplets, tercets, and quatrains, but they do have definite ideas of how poetry means, and how they will write. They do not just scatter words on a page willy-nilly or arrange prose to look like poetry. There is a reason for what they do.

Robert Frost has said that writing free verse is like playing tennis without a net. Other poets would agree with him that to work within set patterns offers a challenge, helps to make us work harder and better toward a good poem. But many poets today feel that metrics or old forms are too confining and do not express our tempo of life. Poets are divided into schools of thought and disagree with each other as to what constitutes a good poem. Many different ideas have been offered. Some believe that poetry should be written like a musical phrase. Some think that each line represents what the poet can say in a single breath. Some call each line they write a single foot. Some compose their poems in short lines and phrases, indicating that the reader must pause after each cluster of words. In this way the white space around a poem becomes a sort of punctuation guide.

One of the first poets who broke from traditional poetry was Walt Whitman. His poetry was free in the sense that it departed from the use of end rhyme. His rhythms, however, are still echoes of the psalms of the Bible, strong in rising and falling rhythms. In a line like

Out of the cradle endlessly rocking,

we find the traditional dactyl-trochee pattern. In

I celebrate myself, and sing myself,

we hear the beat of iambic pentameter. Whitman used a great deal of repetition, internal rhyme, and consonance to create his rhythms.

Others who followed him set up new rules for poetry. Some write their poems with a certain number of stressed syllables in each line. Some count the number of syllables in each line. In her poem "Mushrooms" Sylvia Plath begins

Overnight, very
Whitely, discreetly,
Very quietly

Our toes, our noses
Take hold on the loam,
Acquire the air.

Nobody sees us,
Stops us, betrays us;
The small grains make room. . . .

Count the syllables in each line and you'll discover that there is a regular pattern of five syllables to a line and fifteen to a stanza.

In her poem "Nevertheless" Marianne Moore begins

> you've seen a strawberry
>   that's had a struggle; yet
>   was, where the fragments met,
>
> a hedgehog or a star-
>   fish for the multitude
>   of seeds. What better food
>
> than apple-seeds—the fruit
>   within the fruit—locked in
>   like counter-curved twin
> hazel nuts?

Here Marianne Moore uses six syllables in every line. But did you also notice the rhyming pattern of the tercet (yet/met) (multitude/food) (in/twin)?

In "The Fish" she uses an even more intricate pattern.

> wade
> through black jade.
>   Of the crow-blue mussel-shells, one keeps
>   adjusting the ash-heaps;
>   opening and shutting itself like

an

injured fan.

   The barnacles which encrust the side

   of the wave, cannot hide

      there for the submerged shafts of the

sun, . . .

While this may be difficult for you to read, it shows how she sets up a *syllabic* pattern. Each stanza follows the same pattern of one, three, nine, six, and eight syllables. In addition she has used a rhyming-couplet pattern for the first four lines of each stanza (wade/jade) (keeps/heaps) (an/fan) (side/hide). This is just the beginning of the poem. The pattern continues for six more stanzas!

Arnold Adoff uses white space to indicate to his readers how a poem means. Each word becomes important not only visually, but also to the sense of what he is saying. In *Eats* he writes

Sunny

     side

        up

     bull _s

     eye

     egg

     turn

     over

     easy

       and

     don bre

       t   ak

     the

     yolk.

If you ever hear Arnold Adoff read his poetry, you will discover that each word is meant to be read by itself, the blank space indicating the pause in your voice. Each is also important in considering how a fried egg is cooked. Make sure you heed his warning not to break the yolk, by emphasizing the breaks in the words. Splitting these letters up, let your voice drop as though you yourself are hearing the warning!

In his book *i am the running girl* he sets up

patterns that seem to imitate and underscore the
actual act of running.

              the end

                    is past the tape at the finish line
                    and i am bending to the ground
                                    out of breath
                                    and strength

                    the coach is shouting
                              i have broken   three
                                        minutes
                    for the first time
                    but i am out of
                              time

                        i have no bones
                        i have no legs
                        i have no
                              stomach that will stay
                                    where it began
                    but i have won

Here the phrases, set in separate lines, are written
to represent the way in which the running girl might
be speaking as she crosses the finish line. White
space again indicates where the pauses come. Notice
how often repetition is used here to hold the poem
together.

Lucille Clifton also uses repetition, yet writes her poem "Good Times" with an image in each line, leading us from one picture to another.

> My Daddy has paid the rent
> and the insurance man is gone
> and the lights is back on
> and my uncle Brud has hit
> for one dollar straight
> and they is good times
> good times
> good times
>
> My Mama has made bread
> and Grampaw has come
> and everybody is drunk
> and dancing in the kitchen
> and singing in the kitchen
> oh these is good times
> good times.
> good times
>
> oh children think about the
> good times

The best of open-form poetry is, indeed, more than the license to write down anything you wish. Elements of traditional meter, of sound patterns, of repetition, of syllable count, of word stress, and of rhyme all contribute to how these poems mean.

Those who write well in open forms have learned their craft. They usually know the rules, but they also know how and when they break the rules, and *why!*

If you'd like to try writing in open forms, take time to read other poems that might give you ideas on how to begin. But, by way of a warning, don't make the mistake of thinking that a poem that uses lines of different lengths is necessarily free verse. Many poets (and I am often one of them) like to break up long lines, to make the reader pay attention to certain words, to play with the shape of a poem.

In "Telling Time" Lilian Moore begins

> Time ticks,
> whispers,
> rings,
> sounds a chime,
> a ping,
> a tock,
> or the long slow
> bong
> of a grandfather clock.

At first this would appear to be either a nine-line stanza or even free verse. But reading it aloud, you

will suddenly hear that "tock" in line 6 rhymes with
"clock" in the last line. The poem, then, we recognize
as a quatrain. If written in four lines it would look
like this:

> Time ticks, whispers, rings,
> Sounds a chime, a ping, a tock,
> Or the long slow bong
> Of a grandfather clock.

Its rhythm is largely iambic and anapestic. It is not
free verse but a metered poem using end rhyme.

Another reason for you to always read poetry
aloud!

CONCRETE, SHAPE,
AND PATTERN POETRY

Concrete poetry, often called *pattern poetry* or *shape poetry*, is a form of playing with words, ideas, letters, and art. It is, in a sense, a picture poem, one that gives not only words but delight to the eye.

Sometimes this is accomplished with the outline of a recognizable shape into which words are poured. In Reinhard Döhl's "Pattern Poem with an Elusive Intruder" we see immediately the shape of an apple.

.UI (\p
pfelApfelApfelApte..
,pfelApfelApfelApfelApfe
pfelApfelApfelApfelApfelAp
)felApfelApfelApfelApfelApfe.
elApfelApfelApfelApfelApfelAp
ApfelApfelApfelApfelApfelApfe
ofelApfelApfelApfelApfelApfel/
elApfelApfelApfelApfelApfelAr
pfelApfelApfelApfelApfelApf
elApfelApfelApfelWurmAp'
ofelApfelApfelApfelApfe
lApfelApfelApfelApfe'
felApfelApfelApfr
felApfelAnf

The word for apple in German is *apfel*, which the poet has used over and over to reinforce the idea of the fruit. But if we look very closely we will discover another word, *wurm*, which is German for "worm." This is the "elusive intruder" hiding within!

Look at this concrete poem by Edwin Morgan:

s   sz   sz   SZ   sz   SZ   sz   ZS   zs   ZS   zs   zs   z

Its title, "Siesta of a Hungarian Snake," makes clear that the snake is a long reptile. What amuses us is the use of the letters *s sz sz SZ*, which suggest, as in comic books, the sound of snoring. A siesta is, of course, another name for a nap. The snake is sleeping. But notice that in the middle of the line the sound changes from *sz* to *zs*. This indicates the natural sound of snoring, broken by the way breath may be taken in and out. In addition the consonants *sz* and *zs* are common to the Hungarian language. The meaning of the title is now clear!

In her poem "Concrete Cat" Dorthi Charles not only outlines the shape of a cat, but makes the letters work hard.

A
e ɾ

A
e ɾ

eYe   eYe   stripestripestripestripe
whisker   whisker   stripestripestripe   t
whisker   m   h   whisker   stripestripestripestripes   a   i   l   t   a   i   l
whisker   o   t   whisker   stripestripestripe
          U   stripestripestripestripe

          paw paw   paw paw   ƏSΠOɯ

dishdish   litterbox
                                      litterbox

Notice how the poet has capitalized the *A*, *Y*, and *U* to suggest the shape of the cat's ears, eyes, and mouth. The spaces left between the letters of the word "tail" seem to elongate and emphasize its length. Both words and letters contribute to the fun of the poem. What other details do you notice that might be important to reading this poem?

In her poem "How Everything Happens (Based on a Study of the Wave)" May Swenson imitates in lines the motion of waves coming into shore and going out again.

                                          happen.
                                    to
                                up
                          stacking
                      is
                  something
When nothing is happening

When it happens
              something
                      pulls
                          back
                              not
                                  to
                                  happen.
When   has happened.
      pulling back   stacking up
              happens

          has happened   stacks up.
When it   something   nothing
                          pulls back while

Then nothing is happening.

                                  happens.
                              and
                      forward
                  pushes
              up
          stacks
      something
Then

Robert Froman mixes pictures, shapes, and words in his poems. In "Skyscratcher" he outlines the shape, putting his poem, an apostrophe to the skyscraper, around it.

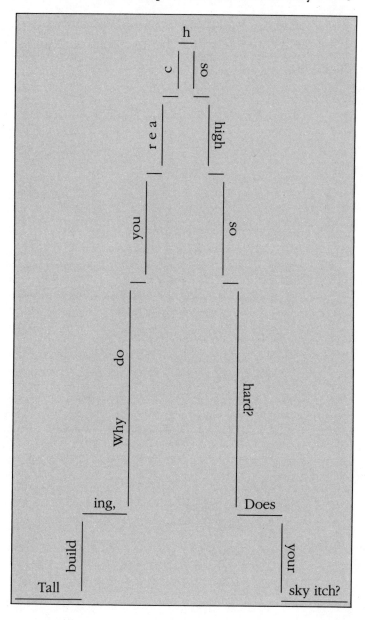

In "Catchers" he again uses drawings, this time of antennas, among which he presents us with a metaphor.

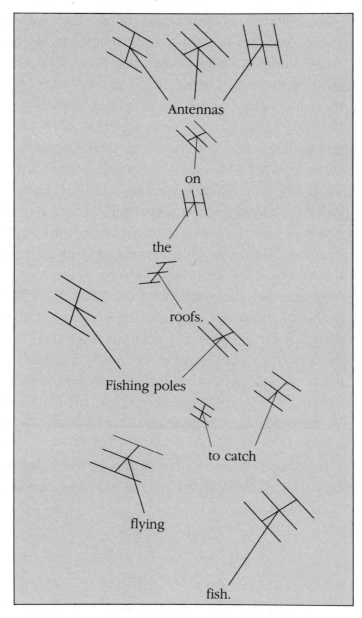

Antennas

on

the

roofs.

Fishing poles

to catch

flying

fish.

It is difficult to say whether or not the idea of shape comes before the words, or whether the words suggest a shape. I have worked both ways. My poem about a Monterey cypress (page 22) was based on the twisted shape of this tree. In a book *Space Songs* I became intrigued with reshaping the words to suggest patterns of a crescent moon, a satellite, or the tail of a comet. One of my first poems, "Buildings," has a long thin stanza suggesting a tall building as well as a quatrain stanza suggesting the shape of a house. For me the words are always more important than the pattern, yet certain words and ideas lend themselves to the making of concrete poetry.

Trying out pattern poetry can be fun. One of the problems, however, is that oftentimes we let the shapes work so hard—place so much attention on the art—that words become secondary. In classes I teach, students often become so involved with a drawing they forget to give meaning to the real idea of their poems. Words merely become an afterthought.

In the best of concrete poetry there should always be a balance between the idea of the poem and its visual expression.

Acknowledgments

Every effort has been made to trace the ownership of all copyrighted material and to secure the necessary permission to reprint these selections. In the event of any question arising as to the use of any material, the editor and publisher, while expressing regret for any inadvertent error, will be happy to make the necessary correction in future printings. Thanks are due to the following for permission to reprint the copyrighted materials listed below:

Joan Aiken for the excerpt from "The Ballad of Newington Green" from her book *The Skin Spinners*, Viking Press, 1976. Copyright © Joan Aiken. Used by permission of the author.

Catherine Beston Barnes for "I Took a Little Stick" by Elizabeth Coatsworth from her book *The Sparrow Bush*, W. W. Norton, 1966. Used by permission.

Carcanet Press Limited for "Siesta of a Hungarian Snake" by Edwin Morgan from his book *Poems of Thirty Years*, 1982.

Laura Cecil for the excerpt from "Tree Gowns." Copyright © James Reeves from *The Wandering Moon and Other Poems* (Puffin Books) by James Reeves. Reprinted by permission of The James Reeves Estate.

Curtis Brown, Ltd., for "July" by Lucille Clifton from *Everett Anderson's Year*, Holt, Rinehart and Winston, 1974. Text Copyright © 1974 by Lucille Clifton. Reprinted by permission of Curtis Brown, Ltd.

Doubleday for "The Ceiling," copyright 1950 by Theodore Roethke. From *The Collected Poems of Theodore Roethke*. Used by permission of Doubleday, a division of Bantam, Doubleday, Dell Publishing Group, Inc.

148 Acknowledgments

from *Out in the Dark and Daylight* by Aileen Fisher. Text copyright © 1980 by Aileen Fisher; text from "There Was a Wet Pig from Fort Wayne" from *The Book of Pigericks: Pig Limericks* by Arnold Lobel. Copyright © 1983 by Arnold Lobel; text from "A Lonely Sparrow" from *Flower Moon Snow: A Book of Haiku* by Kazue Mizumura (Thomas Y. Crowell). Copyright © 1977 by Kazue Mizumura; text from "Aunt Roberta" and the first 3 lines of "Things" from *Honey, I Love* by Eloise Greenfield (Thomas Y. Crowell). Text copyright © 1978 by Eloise Greenfield; and "When I have seen the sun emerge" by Emily Dickinson from *Poems of Emily Dickinson*, selected by Helen Plotz, Thomas Y. Crowell, 1964. All selections reprinted by permission of HarperCollins Publishers.

Harvard University Press for "I Never Saw a Moor" by Emily Dickinson. Reprinted by permission of the publishers and the Trustees of Amherst College from *The Poems of Emily Dickinson*, Thomas H. Johnson, ed., Cambridge, Mass.: The Belknap Press of Harvard University Press, Copyright 1951, © 1955, 1979, 1983 by the President and Fellows of Harvard College.

Henry Holt and Company, Inc., for: 4 lines beginning "Once, when the sky was very near the earth" and ending "her silver necklace," from *The Sun Is a Golden Earring* by Natalia M. Belting. Copyright © 1962 by Natalia M. Belting; and the first 4 lines of "Tree at My Window" from *The Poetry of Robert Frost* edited by Connery Lathem. Copyright 1928, © 1969 by Holt, Rinehart and Winston, © 1956 by Robert Frost. Both reprinted by permission of Henry Holt and Company, Inc.

Houghton Mifflin Company for "It Makes No Difference to Me" from *Doodle Soup* by John Ciardi. Copyright © 1985 by Myra J. Ciardi. Illustrations copyright © 1985 by Merle Nacht. Reprinted by permission of Houghton Mifflin Co.

Olwyn Hughes for the first 9 lines of "Mushrooms" by Sylvia Plath. From *The Collected Poems of Sylvia Plath*, Faber and Faber London. Copyright © 1981 & 1967 by Ted Hughes. Reprinted by permission of Olwyn Hughes.

150 Acknowledgments

Chasing a Hat" from *Something New Begins* by Lilian Moore. Copyright © 1982 by Lilian Moore. Both reprinted with permission of Atheneum Publishers, an imprint of Macmillan Publishing Company. "The Song in My Head" and "The Year" from *The Song in My Head and Other Poems* by Felice Holman. Copyright © 1985 by Felice Holman. Reprinted with permission of Charles Scribner's Sons, an imprint of Macmillan Publishing Company.

William Morrow & Company, Inc., for: "Poor Old Penelope" from *The Queen of Eene* by Jack Prelutsky. Copyright © 1970, 1978 by Jack Prelutsky; "The Lurpp Is on the Loose" from *The Snopp on the Sidewalk* by Jack Prelutsky. Text copyright © 1977, 1978 by Jack Prelutsky. Both by permission of Greenwillow Books, a division of William Morrow & Co., Inc. "Sunny" from *Eats* by Arnold Adoff. Text copyright © 1979 by Arnold Adoff. By permission of Lothrop, Lee & Shepard Books, a division of William Morrow & Co., Inc.

Harold Ober Associates for "The Crow" and "Old Man Ocean" from *The Pedaling Man* by Russell Hoban. Copyright © 1968 by Russell Hoban. Reprinted by permission of Harold Ober Associates Incorporated.

Random House, Inc., for: Excerpt from "Mushrooms" reprinted from *The Colossus and Other Poems* by Sylvia Plath. Copyright © 1960 by Sylvia Plath; "The Warning," "Niagara," and "Winter" from *Verse* by Adelaide Crapsey. Copyright 1922 by Algernon S. Crapsey and renewed 1950 by The Adelaide Crapsey Foundation; "The Brave Man" reprinted from *The Collected Poems of Wallace Stevens*. Copyright 1936 by Wallace Stevens and renewed 1964 by Holly Stevens; "Dreams" and "Poem" from *The Dream Keeper and Other Poems* by Langston Hughes. Copyright 1932 by Alfred A. Knopf Inc. and renewed 1960 by Langston Hughes. All reprinted by permission of Alfred A. Knopf, Inc. "Good Times" from *Good Times* by Lucille Clifton. Copyright © 1969 by Lucille Clifton. Reprinted by permission of Random House Inc. Excerpt from *The Odyssey of Homer*, translated by Robert Fitzgerald. Copyright © 1961, 1963 and renewed 1989 by

Robert Fitzgerald. Reprinted by permission of Vintage Books, a Division of Random House Inc.

Marian Reiner for: "Go Wind" from *I Feel the Same Way*. Copyright © 1967 by Lilian Moore; "Message from a Caterpillar" from *Little Racoon and the Poems from the Woods* by Lilian Moore. Copyright © 1975 by Lilian Moore; Excerpt from "Telling Time" from *Think of Shadows* by Lilian Moore. Copyright © 1975, 1980 by Lilian Moore; "Foghorns" from *I Thought I Heard the City* by Lilian Moore. Copyright © 1969 by Lilian Moore; Excerpt from "Aelourophobe" and "From the Japanese" from *Rainbow Writing* by Eve Merriam. Copyright © 1976 by Eve Merriam; "Metaphor" from *A Sky Full of Poems* by Eve Merriam. Copyright © 1964, 1970, 1973 by Eve Merriam; Excerpt from "Sunset" in *Fresh Paint* by Eve Merriam. Copyright © 1986 by Eve Merriam; "New Notebook" from *Flashlight and Other Poems* by Judith Thurman. Copyright © 1976 by Judith Thurman; "Broken and Broken" (Chosu), "If Things Were Better," "Well! Hello down there," and "What a Pretty Kite" (Issa) and "That duck, bobbing up" (Joso) from *Cricket Songs*, Japanese haiku translated by Harry Behn. Copyright © 1964 by Harry Behn; "A dry leaf drifting" and "The best I have to" (Basho) from *More Cricket Songs*, Japanese haiku translated by Harry Behn. Copyright © 1971 by Harry Behn; "There was once a young fellow of Wall" from *A Lollygag of Limericks* by Myra Cohn Livingston. Copyright © 1978 by Myra Cohn Livingston; "Conversation with Washington" and "Power Lines" from *4-Way Stop and Other Poems* by Myra Cohn Livingston. Copyright © 1976 by Myra Cohn Livingston; "Daddy" (formerly "Leroy") from *No Way of Knowing: Dallas Poems* by Myra Cohn Livingston. Copyright © 1980 by Myra Cohn Livingston; "Garden," "little o," and "T-shirt" from *O Sliver of Liver* by Myra Cohn Livingston. Copyright © 1979 by Myra Cohn Livingston; "Skating Song" from *The Moon and a Star and other Poems* by Myra Cohn Livingston. Copyright © 1965 by Myra Cohn Livingston; "74th Street" from *The Malibu and Other Poems* by Myra Cohn Livingston. Copyright © 1972 by Myra Cohn Livingston; "Discovery" from *Whispers and Other Poems* by Myra Cohn Livingston. Copyright © 1958, 1984 by Myra Cohn Livingston. All are reprinted by permission of Marian Reiner for the authors.

Acknowledgments 153

Norman H. Russell for "Beware of Me!" (Cherokee Indian). Copyright © 1972 by Norman H. Russell. Reprinted by permission of Norman H. Russell.

The Society of Authors for: "The Wind" from *The Collected Poems of James Stephens*, Macmillan, New York, 1927. Reprinted by permission of The Society of Authors on behalf of the copyright owner, Mrs. Iris Wise; "The Snowflake" and excerpts from "The Bees' Song" from *Rhymes and Verses* by Walter de la Mare, Henry Holt, 1947. Reprinted by permission of The Literary Trustees of Walter de la Mare and The Society of Authors as their representative.

The University of California Press for "Song of the Deer" from *Singing for Power: The Song Magic of the Papago Indians of Southern Arizona* by Ruth Underhill. Copyright © 1938, 1966 by Ruth Murray Underhill. Reprinted by permission.

University Press of New England for the first 5 lines of "The Redwoods," copyright © 1960 by Louis Simpson. Reprinted from *At the End of the Open Road* by permission of University Press of New England.

Viking Penguin for "Firefly" and 4 lines from "Strange Tree" from *Under the Tree* by Elizabeth Madox Roberts. Copyright 1922 by B. W. Huebsch, Inc., renewed 1950 by Ivor S. Roberts. Copyright 1930 by The Viking Press, Inc., renewed © 1958 by Ivor S. Roberts and The Viking Press, Inc. Reprinted by permission of Viking Penguin, a division of Penguin Books USA Inc.

Index

155

Index   157

Index

159